'he Vhole Language ɔurney

.RA E. LIPA
:BECCA HARLIN
)SEMARY LONBERGER

ppin Publishing Limited

150 Telson Road
Markham, Ontario
L3R 1E5

Edited by Dyanne Rivers
Designed by John Zehethofer
Printed and bound by the Alger Press

Canadian Cataloguing in Publication Data

Lipa, Sara E., 1937-
The whole language journey

(The Pippin teacher's library ; 3)
Includes bibliographical references.
ISBN 0-88751-034-5

1. Language experience approach in education.
2. Language arts (Elementary). I. Harlin, Rebecca.
II. Lonberger, Rosemary. III. Title. IV. Series.

LB1576.L56 1991 372.6'044 C91-094111-4

ISBN 0-88751-034-5

10 9 8 7 6 5 4 3 2 1

CONTENTS

. . . .

INTRODUCTION

Welcome to the creative, exciting and productive world of whole language. It's a world in which teaching will become even more rewarding and interesting as you observe and interact with children while they learn. It's also a demanding world. To be an effective whole language teacher, it's necessary to understand child development, language development, cooperative learning and reading, writing, listening and speaking at the same time as you model learning for the children and plan and evaluate the learning experiences they will share with you.

The Birth of the Whole Language Movement

During the last decade, teachers throughout the English-speaking world found themselves increasingly frustrated by growing demands that they emphasize instruction in specific skills, presumably to ensure that the children in their care would score well on standardized tests. This would apparently prove that they had indeed been taught reading, writing, listening and speaking. As teachers struggled to meet these demands, imposed in the name of accountability and quality control, they discovered that they had little time to read to or with the children and even less time to write. At the same time, observant teachers began to notice that the very children whose test scores indicated they were "successful" displayed little enjoyment of reading or writing, rarely choosing to do either when given the opportunity. As a result, these teachers began to ask whether their language arts programs were really meeting the needs of the learners in their classrooms.

As teachers began to share their concerns with each other, develop the conviction that change was needed and set out on the search for alternatives, a grass-roots movement started to take shape. Separately, then collectively, they began to say, "There has to be a better way." Small groups of teachers met to explore research in psycholinguistics and process writing, invited speakers to address their questions and brainstormed ways of creating classrooms that fostered literacy through cooperative learning. They encouraged each other to become risk-takers and to begin making changes in their own classroom routines.

They began to schedule time to read aloud to their students and to encourage children to read books for pleasure. Together, teachers and children responded to authors and reacted to plots, instead of focusing on prescribed questions. Teachers began to model the reading process rather than merely assess it. Children were afforded opportunities to draft, revise and share their own writing in environments that supported and encouraged their efforts. As this happened, teachers began to see a change in their own attitudes towards literacy, as well as those of their students. Classroom bookshelves began to fill up with trade and child-authored books that beckoned children to read and reread. In the process, every child was invited to join the "literacy club."

Beginning Your Journey towards Whole Language

If you picked up this book, you are probably interested in becoming a whole language teacher. At this point, however, you may be unsure about how and where to begin.

A logical start is to update your professional knowledge. You need to know something about the whys of whole language before you explore the whats. You might begin by reading current issues of professional journals like *Language Arts, Highway One, The New Advocate, Reading Canada Lecture, Reading, Key Issues, Journal of Research in Reading,* and *The Reading Teacher*. The articles in these journals provide an overview of research in literacy and language development as well as reviews of current children's books.

Another choice is to read professional books that provide in-depth discussions of process writing, whole language theory and literacy development. Because the last 15 years have produced an avalanche of research in all these areas, there is no shortage of sources.

Visiting a whole language teacher support group is another way to begin your journey. Ask other teachers in your building or district where and when various groups meet. Most teacher support groups belong to TAWL (Teachers Applying Whole Language) or CAWL (Children and Whole Language) networks that may help you locate the group in your area. At these meetings, you'll be exposed to classroom-tested ideas as well as lively discussions. Taking time to meet teachers who can help answer your questions is a worthwhile investment.

A third way to begin your journey is to visit a whole language classroom in your building, district or area. This will acquaint you with whole language in action. Making more than one visit may help clarify your thinking and answer some of your logistical questions.

Finally, you might begin by initiating a regularly scheduled time for sharing trade books with your students and discussing their reactions. Keep a log of what you notice during each sharing episode. What changes can you see in the children's responses to the text? How has your own role changed?

Becoming a whole language teacher means investing time in your own development. The time spent reading professional books, attending support group meetings and reading children's books will afford you the background necessary to make informed choices. Whole language teachers evolve over time, trying new approaches and routines and discarding old ones. Each day brings the opportunity to share in the excitement of helping children become independent, literate individuals.

But What about My School?

As every teacher knows, change takes place slowly in schools. You'll need to be patient and persistent in your beliefs that this is, indeed, a better way to teach, as well as knowledgeable about the principles and theories that are the foundation of whole language. Rather than attempting to introduce instant change by asking your principal, headmaster, district superintendent or school board member to endorse whole language before they have seen it in action, try out a few techniques such as shared reading and journal writing. As you and the children become comfortable with various processes, begin to share these techniques with others in your school.

It's always a good idea to share your enthusiasm and ideas with your principal or headmaster. Most will support and encourage your experiments. Invite your supervisors into the classroom to observe first-hand what the children are doing with whole language. Make efforts to find other teachers who share your beliefs and join them in creating a network of ideas for whole language development.

At some point, you may suggest to your principal or headmaster that part of a faculty meeting be devoted to whole language at different grade levels. Like children, adults also learn from each other. Invite other teachers to visit your classroom as well. In one school, staff meetings were held in different classrooms so that the work of the children was shared throughout the faculty.

Most school boards and administrators will support whole language as long as curriculum requirements are met and children are making satisfactory progress. In most whole language classrooms, children and teachers perform well above minimum standards and they do so with enthusiasm and a satisfying sense of achievement.

Finally, be aware that few approaches work 100 percent of the time for everyone and be careful not to discard all traditional practices as irrelevant and inappropriate simply because they have been around for years. Good teaching goes hand-in-hand with good judgment. Current theory suggests that whole language is the appropriate means for teaching children to read and write. But only your leadership will make it happen. Try it, refine it and enjoy helping children achieve literacy in a creative environment.

What Is Whole Language?

The roots of whole language are found in theories setting out how we learn to read. Reading is a complex process requiring readers to bring their own knowledge of language to the printed page, to recognize that print carries meaning-bearing words, sentences and paragraphs and, finally, to interpret an author's message.

These reading acts have been investigated by cognitive and educational psychologists, linguists, sociologists and learning theorists. Each discipline has contributed to our understanding of the triad linking reader, text and author. Whole language theory is based on the contributions of theorists from various disciplines including psycholinguistics, sociolinguistics, developmental and cognitive psychology and cooperative learning theory. Let's take a brief look at how each fits into the whole language mosaic.

PSYCHOLINGUISTICS

By approaching reading as the interaction of language and learning behaviors, psycholinguists have provided a major theoretical base for understanding whole language. For example, they have found that if children have had experiences with planes and helicopters and if their receptive and expressive vocabularies include words such as planes and helicopters, reading about these flying machines will be very easy because their experience and language base will help them make sense of the print. In other words, they will bring their own language, knowledge and experiences to the reading material.

Psycholinguists tell us that readers bring more information *to* the print than they get *from* the print. Experiences become the tools for developing "rules" about learning new information. A major tenet of psycholinguistic theory says that reading is meaningful for us only within the boundaries of our own experiences and language. The text, composed of specific words and sentences, provides only the stimulus for the reader to construct the message.

DEVELOPMENTAL AND COGNITIVE PSYCHOLOGY

The psycholinguistic theory of language and reading development does not completely explain how reading happens. Developmental and cognitive psychologists recognize that, from birth, children move through a growth sequence that includes physical, social, emotional and cognitive development. Before they are ready to learn to crawl, walk, talk and so on, they must have reached the appropriate stage in this developmental sequence.

Physical growth is easily observed as we watch children grow bigger and learn to crawl and walk. At the same time, we know that a tremendous amount of cognitive growth is also occurring as children learn to listen, repeat, remember, categorize, generalize and think in abstract as well as concrete terms. This cognitive growth provides the foundation for learning both oral and written forms of language.

Although guidelines set out the "normal" age for various developmental milestones to occur, every child's rate of development is unique in both quantitative and qualitative terms. Whole language teachers are aware that differences in individual growth patterns will affect how and what children learn during instruction. They know that all the children will not be able to complete the same tasks at the same time, nor will they all act in the same way. Every child is unique, not only in his or her growth patterns, but also in her or his interests and ability to interact with others and learn from experiences. For example, some kindergarten-aged children engage in scribble writing, while others are able to print their names and still others can use "phonic" spelling. Whole language teachers understand these differences in growth and plan instructional sequences to maximize children's learning.

SOCIOLINGUISTICS

Children, as learners, do not interact with an author, an adult or other children unless it is within a meaningful, sociolinguistic context. Talk, play and role-playing are the social settings that allow children to practice various forms of communication. The social context provides a meaning and reason to communicate.

Children learn best when they are encouraged to participate in an event, contribute to a social situation or be part of a "community" such as a class or a small group. For example, children in kindergarten might play "grocery store." You'll hear them talking about their grocery lists, why they'll buy oat bran instead of *Froot Loops* and healthy snacks such as apples instead of candy. One child might role-play the clerk, another the butcher and a third the customer. As they mimic the kind of talk heard in grocery stores, they are increasing their understanding of the differing attitudes towards and purposes for grocery shopping.

By contrast, a small group of sixth graders might be intent on developing a bulletin board display about a series of stories they've read by one author. The social context becomes the small group working on the bulletin board project. The focus of their work is to complete the project and their talk reflects this purpose as each student contributes suggestions and information.

Whole language teachers understand that events such as reading aloud a big book, listening to authors and readers, providing for peer revision of children's compositions and sharing ideas for social studies and science projects make up the social contexts of the classroom. Each of these activities requires children to use language for different purposes — to question, comment, explain or clarify. These contexts provide the setting for language communication and reading development at home, at school and within the community.

COOPERATIVE LEARNING

Cooperative learning theory stresses the importance of group members helping each other. Children often learn best from each other. Let's listen in, for example, on the sixth graders at work on the bulletin board project mentioned previously.

John suggests to Diane, "How about you and me doing the illustrations for the books we've read?" Jean volunteers, "Matt and I will do a summary of *The Cay*. We liked different parts of the story so our summary will interest different kids." Martha, who has a different idea, says, "I think it would be interesting if we all helped make a story map about *The Cay*. If we combine our ideas, I bet it'll turn out really well. I'll write down the ideas as we think of them. We can do the editing later." Falling in with this idea, John says, "*The Cay* is about people shipwrecked on an island." Ray chimes in with, "I agree but don't you think we should say who was shipwrecked?" Joan wants to talk about the message. She says, "Right, but isn't it really about people helping each other survive?"

The give-and-take involved in stating ideas and adding and refining information while working together is the hallmark of a cooperative learning environment. The talk of these sixth graders is based on the common experience of reading the same book. They now have the opportunity to discuss and act on this experience by expressing their feelings about and interpretations of it with other group members.

Activities like these allow students to select their own level of participation and feel confident about their contribution. Their involvement in the group discussion sparks the creation of many more ideas than might otherwise surface. Because they "own" their learning, it is both meaningful and lasting. Cooperative learning groups provide opportunities for sharing information, clarifying ideas and answering questions in language children readily understand because it is their own. The differences in the their level of expertise and knowledge means each person contributes a unique strength that helps all members of the group learn and understand new information. Whole language teachers create the social setting for cooperative learning by encouraging individuals to work in groups.

LISTENING, SPEAKING, READING AND WRITING IN A WHOLISTIC CONTEXT

In whole language classrooms, listening, speaking, reading and writing are treated as integrated, inseparable elements of language, not discrete subjects that must be taught separately.

For a long time, we've known that speech develops naturally in children. Psycholinguists tell us that young children learn to use language wholistically because they have learned that certain words, phrases and sentences will tell, direct or ask something. They are not required to master the rules for communicating in English before they're allowed to try saying complete words. Rather, their early, imperfect attempts at speech are praised and encouraged by doting parents. As young children listen to adults and other children, practice saying individual sounds such as Mama and Dada, mimic speech patterns they have heard and refine their own attempts to talk, they are learning to derive meaning from the speech of others and use speech themselves.

Because reading springs from a system of writing in which symbols represent the sounds of spoken English, whole language theorists believe that knowledge of oral language transfers to understanding how written language works and that language instruction in school should be an extension of the natural learning that happens before children enter school.

Linguists have studied the development of language and highlighted some milestones. Oral language stages such as babbling, holophrase (saying one word), telegraphic speech (saying two or more words), sentence production and, finally, using simple and complex grammatical structures appear to develop similarly among most children.

By the time children enter school, most of the sentence constructions used by adults are present in their oral speech. Their ability to understand and decode written language appears to develop along similar lines. Recent research has shown that young children start by making scribble marks on their papers. This scribble stage of writing has been compared to the babble stage of acquiring oral language. As children learn to form letters, they use these letters in different combinations to "write" different words. This stage can be compared to the whole-word stage in the development of oral language. For example, Jenny might write *neJ* for mother, *enjn* for dad and *Jn* for Jenny. There appears to be an implicit understanding that arranging letters in different combinations is important for communicating. Just as children learn to talk in phrases and sentences, so they learn to write using the English sound system. We might see Jenny writing about a trip to the zoo this way: *Jn wt 2 z* — Jenny went to the zoo. Later, she will refine this system to include vowels, some of them correct and some attempted — *Jeny wet to th zu*. Finally, she will refine her spelling system to conform to that of standard English — *Jenny went to the zoo.*

Beginning readers have already acquired an oral language base. They understand the purposes for speaking and can change their speech patterns to fit different social situations. In fact, children can anticipate what is written in storybooks if they have had exposure to stories before entering school. Learning to read involves learning to "map" (point to words as they are read) spoken language with written language, to identify print as a written form of words, phrases and sentences and understand the printed message. This learning can occur naturally as long as language patterns in books are similar to those of children's own language, the teacher takes enough time to repeat stories over and over, children are given an opportunity to work with peers to "figure out" the meaning of the print, and, as teachers, we are not overly concerned about the correctness of each word the children say. Just as oral language takes time to learn, so, too, does reading. Providing children with opportunities to practice, imitate, share information with peers and make errors in word identification encourages them to learn to read naturally, the same way they learned to speak.

Although the patterns of language development are similar among children, the rate at which they learn language is regulated by individual differences. When some children enter school, they have already had rich experiences with print in their homes. These children have been read to regularly. They know many stories so well that they will correct an adult if the story isn't read exactly as it was before. They have also had many opportunities to express themselves at home. They are comfortable with school language, attending to directions and using language socially as well as informatively.

Other children have not had the advantage of engaging in activities like this. They will need opportunities to build their own repertoire of language experiences. Because they know that no two children enter school possessing the same literacy information or the same learning rate, background and social experiences, whole language teachers take these differences into account when they are planning classroom programs.

In summary, whole language philosophy draws from many theories to suggest that literacy is best developed by integrating the learning of language (reading, writing, speaking and listening) with theories about child learning, social development and cooperative learning. This book, then, is about one goal of schooling — developing literacy for all children in a natural way.

. . . .

LAY THE GROUNDWORK

Whole language teachers are not a homogeneous group. While they may share a wholistic philosophy, this often shows up in their classrooms in unique ways. Schedules differ, classroom environments vary and personal teaching styles affect the way whole language principles are incorporated into daily routines. Nevertheless, one thing is certain — all whole language teachers have made a commitment to be life-long readers and writers. They're also committed to learning. They realize the importance of keeping abreast of current theories about and research relating to language development. They forever seek to improve their teaching by trying new strategies.

Professional Reading

Wading through the myriad of books and journal articles on whole language can be confusing. Titles are occasionally misleading and sometimes a book purchased with limited funds doesn't live up to its billing. The problem then becomes, "Where do I start?"

To help you sort through this abundance of material, we have included a bibliography of professional resources starting on p. 87. To enable you to select readings that meet your current needs, this includes synopses of recommended books as well as references to journal articles and videotapes likely to be helpful to emergent whole language teachers. The listings are organized under headings that represent topics of major interest in the field. In the sense that all the materials mentioned are wholistic, presenting the language arts as interrelated and integrated across the curriculum, these divisions are somewhat arbitrary. Many titles could have been listed under more than one heading.

Remember, the whole language philosophy empowers teachers to take control of their own classrooms. Professional resources provide ideas to be tried, reworked and molded to fit individual needs. They are not intended, and should not be used, as recipe books that must be followed precisely for fear of spoiling the final product. That's one of the nice things about whole language . . . there is no "final product." Whole language classrooms are always changing to incorporate the latest developments in language learning.

PROFESSIONAL RESOURCES AS AN IMPETUS FOR CHANGE

Your interest in whole language may have evolved because your intuition told you that children can learn to read and write when they have a real purpose for doing so. Or perhaps your perception of how children learn was at odds with your classroom practices. Perhaps you were concerned because your students can read, but choose not to. Or maybe the hoopla over whole language sparked your curiosity and you decided to do some first-hand exploring.

Whatever the reason, your interest probably began with questions. This inquiry is the first step in your journey towards whole language, a cyclical process that gradually integrates newly acquired knowledge into your classroom practices. The stages of this process involve asking questions, locating professional resources, reflecting on these resources, implementing the ideas, observing the effects, reflecting on your observations and then asking more questions that spark the cycle to begin again.

The first stage in the cycle, the point at which you began to ask questions, has been labeled transitional inquiry. The most important aspect of this entry-level step is that you own it. This means that you formulate your own questions, which probably reflect your interests as well as your perception of your immediate needs, and answer them in a way that feels comfortable. Some teachers decide to begin by acquiring a basic understanding of whole language theory, while others rely on their intuition about how children learn and begin by locating strategies in line with their beliefs.

The second stage of the process, locating professional resources, involves finding information to help address your queries or refine your initial questions. Professional resources include books, journal articles, videotapes, whole language support groups and colleagues who share similar interests.

Let's look at how you might integrate these resources. Suppose you're a primary teacher who has been growing increasingly uncomfortable with your program, which presents reading as a set of skills. Because many children appear confused about or bored by lessons that involve introducing a new letter-sound each week, you're beginning to sense that the process has little meaning for them. At the same time, you've heard about the shared book experience and wonder if this might meet the children's needs. You begin to seek out readings that will provide more information about this approach.

Using the synopses provided in the bibliography of this book as a guide, you decide to read Donald Holdaway's *The Foundations of Literacy* to improve your understanding of the theoretical underpinnings of shared reading, Priscilla Lynch's *Using Big Books and Predictable Books* to grasp the practical aspects of implementing the procedure, and view the videotape, *A Day in the Life of Mrs. Wishy Washy*, for one teacher's first-hand account of how things work in a real classroom.

Once you've done these things, it's time to reflect on your newly acquired knowledge. Which aspects of shared reading fit into your current situation? Which need adaptation? What further questions do you have? What further information do you need before you'll feel comfortable incorporating the procedure? At this stage, you need to analyze yourself as a learner and address your specific needs. Perhaps you'll feel more comfortable viewing another videotape, observing a colleague or reading a specific journal article before starting something new.

Once you're comfortable with your knowledge base, it's time to move on to the implementation stage. Plan your strategy and begin. Keep your objectives in mind and take ownership of the situation. Observe what happens and, when you feel comfortable, invite others to observe too. Listen to the children. How do they feel about what's happening? Collect and examine examples of their work. Keep a journal describing what happened and record your observations on audio or videotape, if you wish. It's important to examine the teaching-learning situation, to turn it inside out and ask what worked and what didn't so that the necessary adaptations are incorporated into your activities next time round.

This process is cyclical and self-generating, with the anomalies you observe this time inspiring new inquiries, which then serve as an impetus for acquiring and reflecting upon new knowledge. Again this is translated into instructional practice, which is then reflected and improved upon the next time round. Throughout the process, be patient with yourself. Change comes gradually. Don't feel compelled to do it all — or do it all perfectly — right off the bat.

PROFESSIONAL RESOURCES AS AN IMPETUS FOR COLLABORATION

Your colleagues, other teachers interested in whole language, can provide an important sounding board for clarifying and extending ideas acquired through professional readings. Discussions can take place in a variety of contexts, whether they are a regular feature of TAWL group meetings or simply crop up in casual conversation with another teacher.

Formal discussion groups can be structured in a variety of ways. It often works well if one of the participants acts as convener and another as notetaker. The discussion may focus on a single reading, a selection of articles, each of which has been read by everyone in the group, or a series of readings on the same theme from which each group member has chosen one title.

Creating Classrooms for Authors: The Reading-Writing Connection provides an excellent model for organizing a discussion group. If each participant, in turn, shares what she or he read and learned, an open discussion can follow. It's important, at this stage, for participants to feel comfortable asking questions to clarify the information presented. They should also feel free to relate information drawn from the readings and the ensuing discussion to their own classroom experiences and to talk about the instructional implications of their new knowledge. As group members begin to apply in their own classrooms the strategies discussed, they may wish to share their reflections, students' work and so on at a subsequent meeting. Remember, learning is a collaborative enterprise and discussion groups are an important part of your learning community.

PROFESSIONAL RESOURCES AS AN IMPETUS FOR CLASSROOM RESEARCH

In *Whole Language: Inquiring Voices*, Dorothy Watson, Carolyn Burke and Jerome Harste describe research as a "formalized version of teaching." They contend that inquiry is natural to all learners, requiring no special talents.

While research is often perceived as a quantitative endeavor performed by skilled experts under controlled conditions, with limited implications for classroom practice, the whole language movement highlights the importance of research carried out by teachers for teachers and, in so doing, ensures that classroom teachers are recognized as legitimate researchers.

Watson, Burke and Harste provide many suggestions for budding teacher-researchers. One of these is to write a vignette describing the scene in your classroom during a particularly satisfying part of your program. Then note one or two things you'd like to add or change. As you make these changes, document each stage of the process. This includes collecting samples of students' work and making anecdotal records, observational notes, videotapes, audiotapes of classroom interactions and so on. Devise a system for measuring change, collect, analyze and interpret the data, and determine the educational implications of what you've learned.

Anomalies, deviations that occur in classrooms when, for example, things that are expected to work don't, provide another opportunity for research. When an anomaly is identified, the sensitive teacher responds by observing closely and collecting as much information as possible. If the anomaly continues to exist, it may be necessary to revise the initial pattern or formulate an entirely new plan to address the concerns that arise from it.

No matter what the impetus, every time a teacher poses a question and systematically attempts to answer it, he or she is conducting a form of research. Whole language teachers integrate knowledge obtained from books with knowledge obtained in their own classrooms to enhance student learning.

Whole Language in Action

For many teachers, the theory and practice they've read about in books and articles or heard about at seminars and workshops are clarified through visits to classrooms where they can view whole language strategies in action. To maximize the benefits of a visit like this, you need to know what to look for, how to schedule your visit to allow enough time for both observation and conversation with the teacher, and how to use the information gathered.

PLAN YOUR VISIT

What do you look for in a whole language classroom? After reading about this approach, you probably have a pretty good idea of how whole language classrooms operate — in theory. At the same time, you probably have lots of questions about how the theory is actually applied.

Your first task is to select a site for your visit. You'll likely decide to visit a classroom where the children are at the same grade level and from roughly the same background as the youngsters you teach. Consider your priorities. Do you want to observe a classroom where the teacher is well-experienced in applying whole language theory or one where she or he is just setting out? If you choose the former, many of the processes and routines you've read about may already be in place, providing an opportunity to clarify information gained from your reading. If you select the latter, you may gain valuable pointers that will help you decide where to start. Once your priorities are set, contact a whole language support group for a list of teachers in your area. Addresses are listed in the bibliography.

With your list in hand, write to several teachers requesting information about their classrooms and the children they teach, their experience with whole language and their willingness to host a visit. Be sure to indicate that you would like to set the stage with a half-hour meeting beforehand and that you plan to observe for at least a morning, although a day is preferable. You should also plan a half-hour meeting with the teacher at the end of your visit to ask questions and debrief.

These three elements — setting the stage, observing and debriefing — will help make the most of your visit. You'll begin with a context for your observations, know what routines were established and how and, at the end of the day, have an opportunity to ask questions and clear up any misunderstandings about the processes and practices observed.

THE CLASSROOM ENVIRONMENT

The day has finally arrived! A whole language teacher has agreed to your visit and you've taken your place in the classroom. To capture your impressions accurately, you may decide to take notes, draw diagrams, use a checklist similar to the example in Appendix 1 or take photos — with the teacher's permission, of course.

Because whole language classrooms are child-centered, rather than teacher-centered, one of the first things you're likely to notice is the classroom environment. What, for example, do you notice about the arrangement of furniture? The children may be seated at tables or desks grouped in clusters of four or six. An arrangement like this usually implies that they are encouraged to work cooperatively and share ideas. Quiet areas are separated from noisier ones. Beanbag chairs, carpet squares, a rocking chair or comfortable floor pillows may invite children to relax and read books for pleasure in one corner while centers for writing, arts and crafts and experimenting with science and math materials are located in adjacent areas. Every inch of space is well used.

How are materials organized, stored and displayed? Books, children's magazines, encyclopedias, dictionaries, atlases, thesauruses and manipulatives should be readily accessible. The teacher may use cubbyholes, bookshelves, baskets, trays or corrugated boxes to avoid clutter. Play areas and centers should have books and writing materials available for the children while they work. Are storage areas labeled so children can replace materials when they're not in use?

Whole language classrooms contain a variety of commercially published materials as well as books the children and teacher have created together. What children's products are evident — paintings, drawings, writing, child-authored books and charts? How is print used and displayed? Are the children's drawings labeled? You should be able to see how the teacher and children created their literate environment.

Before the children arrive, ask for a copy of the teacher's schedule. It should be apparent that time has been scheduled throughout the day for whole class, small group and individual reading and writing activities. Whole language teachers usually devote large blocks of time to literacy activities rather than scheduling separate bits and pieces for instruction in spelling, handwriting, phonics, composition, reading and grammar. In many whole language classrooms, teachers allot 20 to 30 percent of their time for direct instruction and 70 to 80 percent for students to engage in independent or group activities.

Teachers' schedules often reflect their familiarity with literature-based reading and process writing. Experienced whole language teachers use conferences and workshops for reading and writing while those with less experience often rely more on teacher-directed activities. During their first year of implementing whole language, four first-grade teachers developed this schedule.

Morning Schedule

15 minutes — Whole Class Shared Reading
100 minutes — Group and Individual Work as Indicated

Group A	Group B
20 min. Teacher Instruction	20 min. Creative Response
15 min. Independent Reading	20 min. Teacher Instruction
20 min. Creative Response	15 min. Independent Reading
15 min. Free Reading	30 min. Writing/Journals
30 min. Writing/Journals	15 min. Free Reading
Group C	**Group D**
30 min. Writing/Journals	15 min. Free Reading
15 min. Free Reading	20 min. Creative Response
20 min. Teacher Instruction	30 min. Writing/Journals
15 min. Independent Reading	20 min. Teacher Instruction
20 min. Creative Response	15 min. Independent Reading

The last 15 minutes are used for teacher observation.

At the beginning of every day, the whole class gathered with the teacher for shared reading. The children then moved on to do individual and group work. When they weren't engaged in direct instruction with the teacher, they reread books used for instruction alone or with a partner (independent reading), responded to texts read during shared or individual reading through art, drama, writing or puppetry (creative response), selected and read a book for pleasure (free reading), and wrote drafts or journal entries (writing). During the morning, the teacher had an opportunity to work with individual children, informally evaluate students and monitor each group. A balance was maintained between direct instruction and independent reading and writing.

This timetable shows how a more experienced teacher might organize a school day.

Daily Schedule

8:00 - 8:30	Opening Exercises Journal Writing and Sharing
8:30 - 8:45	Class News Chart Story/Language Experience (Science or social studies topic)
8:45 - 9:30	Mathematics — Centers, Practice Activities (Small group work with teacher — groups rotate for 15-minute sessions)
9:30 - 9:45	Mini Writing Lesson with Whole Class (Focus on one skill or strategy)
9:45 -10:45	Writer's Workshop and Conferences (Children's drafts and teacher's observations)
10:45 -11:35	Art, Music, Physical Education, Library
11:35 -12:25	Lunch
12:25 -12:40	Teacher Reads Theme Story to Class
12:45 - 1:05	Shared Reading with Whole Class (Based on current theme or topic)
1:05 - 1:50	Small Group Reading and Creative Activities (15-minute sessions — teacher's instructional group, arts, crafts, blocks, sand and water table, paper center)
1:50 - 2:10	Sustained Silent Reading Time (SSRT)
2:10 - 2:20	Reading Response Logs (Individuals respond to SSRT books)
2:20 - 2:30	Clean-Up and Review of Day

As you can see, this teacher also uses whole class, individual and small group activities while balancing direct instruction with independent work. However, the schedule reflects this teacher's greater experience with process writing.

As teachers schedule their day's activities, curriculum mandates set out by various agencies are considered. One way of developing literacy while meeting the objectives of these mandates and addressing the content demands of science, social studies and mathematics is to integrate topics through literature study, writing and themes.

The second schedule meets these objectives by using a science or social studies theme as the basis for selecting both the books for shared reading and those available for sustained silent reading, the topic for the language experience chart and the subject that provides the focus for writing workshops. The children become literate and develop facility with language while learning about a topic in depth.

If separate subject areas such as science or social studies do not appear on the daily schedule of the classroom you chose to visit, ask how these are addressed.

MOVEMENT

What do you notice about the transition from one activity to the next? Is there a logical flow from teacher-directed instruction to small group or independent work? Do the children seem aware of the routines and where to go next?

If you expected to find 25 children sitting in rows, working silently, you're probably in for a surprise. Whole language teachers recognize that literacy is a developmental process requiring hands-on experiences, active participation and talk while learning. Throughout the day, you'll see children moving about purposefully as they engage in activities involving reading, writing, listening and speaking. If you listen carefully, you should find that the children's talk focuses on the task at hand — sharing a written draft with their peers, suggesting improvements to another author, responding to a shared book, planning a model or conducting an experiment.

Whole language classrooms are usually arranged to allow children and their teacher ample space for activities and to facilitate a flow of traffic that enables easy transitions from one activity to the next. As you watch the teacher and children

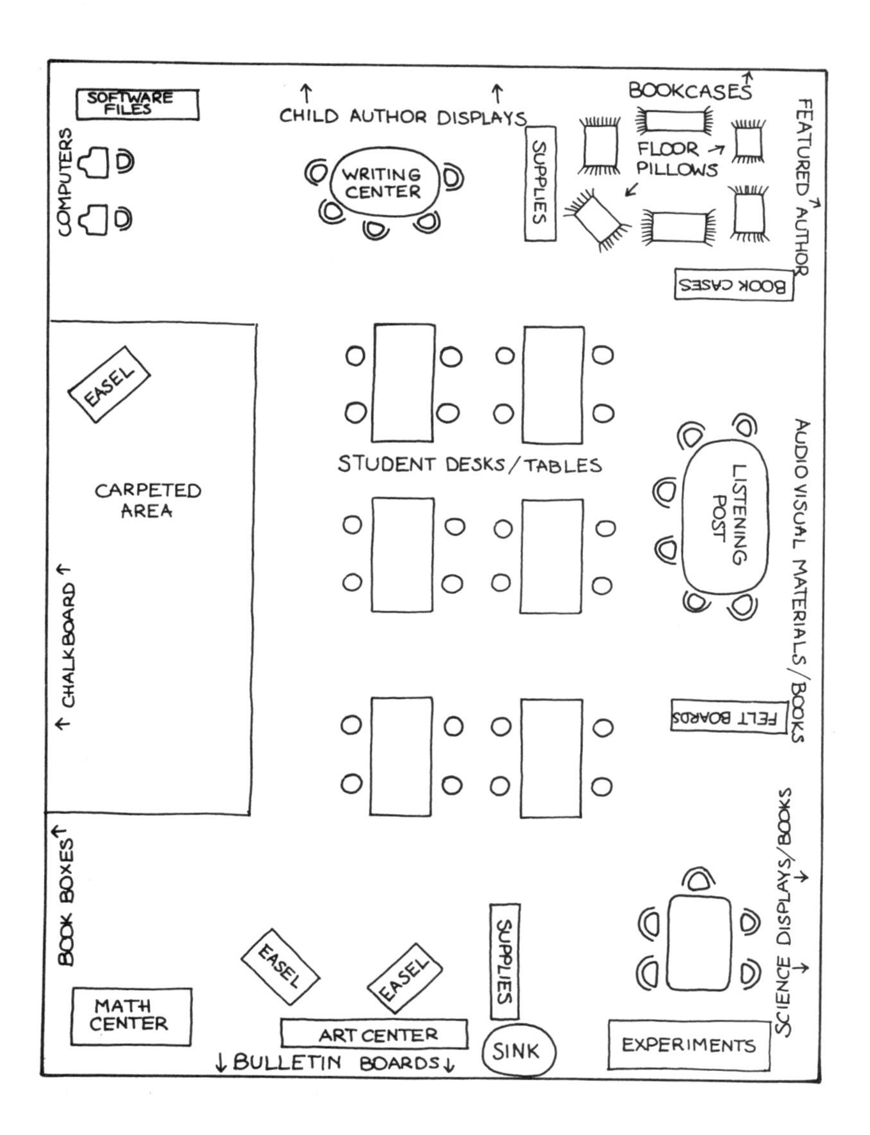

function, it should be apparent that the environment is conducive to exploration, experimentation and social interaction.

If you examine this diagram of one whole language classroom, you'll notice that furniture such as desks, tables and bookshelves is positioned to create a traffic flow that directs movement away from quiet areas. Bookshelves serve double duty — to buffer the reading area and display the featured author's works. Desks are grouped to provide large work surfaces for writing and group projects. Children working at the computer or science center are not interrupted as others travel to and from the pencil sharpener or water fountain. Supplies are stored near activity centers for accessibility.

How does the classroom you're visiting compare to the diagram? During your visit, you might make a point of watching one or two children as they change activities to see how well the traffic flow works. What happens when they are in a teacher-directed activity? A small group activity? An independent activity? Children should be able to move from one activity to the next as quickly as possible with minimal difficulty.

You may be interested in how the teacher familiarized her children with the routines of the centers, reading corners and hands-on activities and how she helped them develop independent work habits. Experienced whole language teachers have established routines that facilitate movement and address the logistical considerations of moving 25 or 30 students through the school day.

INTERACTION

Perhaps one of the most striking contrasts between whole language and traditional classrooms is found in the quality of interaction between the teacher and students. Whole language teachers recognize that to learn language, either oral or written, children must use it. Many opportunities for them to talk to each other and the teacher about books, their own writing or a topic of interest are built into the program. The teacher's method of interacting with students is more like what goes on in the "real world" outside the school than that of traditional teachers. Whole language teachers ask children what they thought of an author's writing, how they liked the characters and whether the plot was believable. They treat the students' language with respect and respond to their intended meaning.

As you observe children's interactions with books, you may also notice a difference in their focus. As the teacher shares a big book, they may, for example, offer predictions, comment spontaneously about the print or point out a feature of an illustration. Notice how the teacher introduces a book that is going to be read aloud, especially one that may be too difficult for the children to read on their own. How are the children encouraged to respond when the reading ends? Some children may compare characters from different books, for example, while others may comment on the author's dialogue.

During recreational reading, what do children say to their peers? You may find the children's comments resemble those made by adults when they discuss books. Most children clarify what they do and don't like about a book, character or author. Their comments may indicate the development of taste in literature as they begin to recognize which authors include humor, authentic-sounding dialogue and believable storylines. Some children decide to emulate a favorite book or author as they compose their own stories.

You may overhear a conversation like this one that took place in Mrs. Davis's classroom, where nine-year-olds enjoy reading for pleasure. Sarah and Jenny had just finished reading *The Polar Express* by Chris Van Allsburg.

Sarah looked at Jenny and said, "Wow! That was a good story." Jenny replied, "Yeah. I liked it better than *Jumanji,* didn't you?" After thinking for a moment, Sarah said, "Well, I liked them both. They made you wonder if things really happened or if the kids just imagined everything. I like the way Chris Van Allsburg lets you make up your own mind. He doesn't tell you what to think."

Teacher's Role

In whole language classrooms, teachers are models and facilitators. They support the children's language and literacy development by providing a role model. They show children what a reader does by sharing books they're reading for pleasure, talking about authors and modeling ways to select books. When the children are reading for pleasure, whole language teachers don't patrol the room or mark papers. They, too, read books of their own choosing, clearly sending the message that reading for pleasure is important. It must be if it's scheduled for children and the teacher, too!

The same is true of writing. When the children write in journals, whole language teachers also record their own daily entries. To encourage the children to be risk-takers, teachers are the first to read their entries to the class and elicit responses. They model how they developed their own topic list and discuss where they got their ideas.

In her classroom of 10-year-olds, for example, Mrs. Scanlin demonstrated how she came up with her a list of writing ideas by saying, "Today, I'm going to show you how an author develops a list of potential topics from her hobbies, experiences, favorite things and pet peeves. At the top of my list is snorkeling because it's a sport I enjoy whenever I'm near warm water. Next is bicycling — I usually ride after school to relax. Chocolate is also on my list because it's my favorite food. Collies belong on my list because I've owned several and have learned quite a bit about this breed. I'm also including slow drivers since this is something that annoys me and I could write about how they make me feel when I follow them. Hawaii is another of my topics because I've vacationed on different islands and could share what I've found on each one. Since I can write best about what I know, my topic list will help me focus on ideas and develop my drafts. As I learn new things or develop new interests, I'll add to my list. Now let's spend some time developing your topic lists."

As children share their drafts, Mrs. Scanlin models the appropriate way to respond to an author — how to offer suggestions, ask questions and indicate a need for more information without overwhelming the child author with too much to do. Instead of just telling children to *be* writers, she shows them what a writer does.

Whole language classrooms are environments designed by teachers to facilitate learning about and using language in many contexts. Whole language teachers also facilitate literacy through direct instruction, discussions and hands-on experiences.

Direct instruction in whole language classrooms may take several forms. In reading, for example, the teacher may invite the children to participate in oral or written cloze activities.

Completing a chart comparing different versions of a folktale such as *Jack and the Beanstalk* is an activity that can spark all sorts of discussions and continue for several days. As each book is read, children list the characters, the setting, the items that were reclaimed from the giant, the solution to the problem and the ending of the tale. Similarities and differences among versions become obvious as each description is completed. Among themselves, the children decide how these differences affect their view of Jack and the giant. They also notice that the original owner of the valuables is made clear in some versions, but left up in the air in others. Through discussion, they draw their own conclusions about whether Jack is justified in claiming the property.

In a class discussion, the children might debate whether the giant was wronged. Next, the teacher and children identify elements they disliked in each version and discuss how the story could be improved. With much enthusiasm, they plan their own version, deciding to set the story in a present-day city. Together they create a text that satisfies everybody. After revisions are made, their version is typed, illustrated and "published" and placed in the classroom library. Throughout the project, the children's understanding of folktales was extended as they read, listened to, discussed and wrote about each version.

In writing, direct instruction may take the form of mini-lessons, like those indicated on the second teacher's schedule. These 15-minute lessons, which focus on a single aspect of the writing process, are geared to the students' needs, not to the order of chapters in a language arts textbook.

After observing where children experienced difficulty as they worked on their own writing, the teacher selects one aspect of writing as the focus for a mini-lesson. The skill or strategy is demonstrated in the context of a text, usually one the teacher has written or something an anonymous student has consented to share. If the focus is punctuation at the end of sentences, for example, the teacher might project the draft onto a screen, read it as written and punctuated and invite comments. Next she might model how to determine natural sentence boundaries by reading the draft aloud and noticing where pauses occur. Alternative ways of punctuating sentences would be offered and read aloud to train students to use their "ear" for language as well as their "eye."

Discussions in whole language classrooms underscore the responsibilities for learning shared by teacher and students. Whether the focus is on a book or a topic in science, teachers are not expected to carry the ball or answer their own questions. They plan discussions carefully to include questions or comments that will invite students to offer alternative responses and solutions. In situations like this, students are not playing the game of school, gearing their responses to what they perceive is the teacher's idea of the correct answer. Open-ended questions encourage students to respond with thoughtful answers, regardless of their age. They know they are expected to think and to share their interpretations and criticisms.

In discussing *Goldilocks and the Three Bears*, for example, the teacher is more likely to ask what the outcome might be for Goldilocks if the story were set in the present day — would she be considered a vandal and subjected to prosecution? — than to inquire what piece of furniture she destroyed. When a new topic is introduced in science or social studies, children may be asked to brainstorm questions they would like to answer or share what they already know. In this way, teachers help children develop a personal investment in their learning.

Teachers ask questions like, "What do you want to learn about _____?" or "How could we find out how ____ works?" As the children research a topic or conduct an experiment, they are encouraged to share their findings with others. Together, teachers and children consider what they have learned and what still needs to be investigated. The discussions, like the children's investigations, are authentic. As you observe the teacher, take special note of the questions asked and the pattern of discussions with students.

Hands-on experiences play an important role in whole language learning. Children need time to experiment, observe, manipulate and play. With each experience, language is developed and extended through writing, reading, talking and listening as children interact with the task and each other. Words are added to children's vocabularies as they engage in meaningful activities. For example, the meaning of words like buoyant and submerge is clarified as children experiment with objects that sink or float.

With these things in mind, whole language teachers structure and coordinate the centers in the classroom. Their role is to introduce the routines of the center or activity, set expectations and encourage children to interact with the activities. They help youngsters make choices and move from one area to the next while monitoring their progress as they do so. Teachers need to set realistic expectations and reasonable time limits for children to complete their tasks. Learning how to plan these experiences takes time and timetables are likely to undergo frequent revisions during the early going.

As you observe, you may begin to appreciate the knowledge of children, literacy and developmental learning possessed by effective whole language teachers. Like you, they started changing their traditional routines slowly, trying out ideas they had read or heard about, evaluating their appropriateness in light of the children's responses and the constraints imposed by the school or district administration, and considering where to go next. While they didn't always know they were right, they did know when an idea was successful!

Whole language programs, like the teachers' knowledge base, evolved over time. During your debriefing, you may ask how the teacher got started and where she or he intends to go next.

Students' Roles

Whether they are six or 10 years old, children in whole language classrooms have an investment and an interest in their learning. They share in the decision-making through, for example, voting on authors to study, suggesting projects to undertake and setting their own goals as readers and writers. Because everyone is encouraged to be an active participant in literacy, children feel a sense of belonging and learn to work responsibly and independently.

In reading, children are expected to choose the books they read for pleasure and experiment with different genres and authors. A steady diet of *Curious George* or *The Babysitter's Club* is unlikely to last. Children learn to talk about books with each other and the teacher. They learn to recommend books to their friends as well as how to express their opinions when the recommended book didn't live up to expectations.

In reading workshops, children may maintain response logs in which they conduct a written dialogue with the teacher about the books they are reading. As they read independently or with a partner, they have the opportunity to apply word-recognition strategies modeled by the teacher and to become effective readers as they make predictions about what will happen next.

In writing, children are in charge of their own topic lists, which form the basis for much of the writing they will do. It is their responsibility to update this list periodically as they learn and study in science, social studies and mathematics. During writing workshops, children are expected to focus on ideas, the audience for and the purpose of their writing. They are usually allotted about 30 minutes to work on their drafts and additional time to confer with peers and receive feedback.

During peer conferences, the children listen to the author as the draft is read, respond to what they like, request clarification and offer suggestions for changes. Because children know they will have their own turn to share, they learn to respond appropriately and kindly to the efforts of their classmates. Revision strategies as well as editing techniques are applied as children improve their drafts. Inside their folders is a list of editing and revising skills that can be applied independently and they are expected to do so. Celebrating the final publication of a piece of writing is an enjoyable reward for most children. They learn to be writers just as they learned to be readers — by doing it!

In whole language classrooms, children are responsible for helping maintain the reading corner, classroom library and centers. Materials are organized after use and supplies are replenished as needed. Whether they are working independently, with a partner or in a group, children learn how to complete a task or solve a problem themselves. Brainstorming, researching and trying alternative solutions become natural responses when problems are presented.

While no two whole language classrooms are exactly alike, the element common to all is the child-centered learning environment. Does the classroom you're observing appear to be child-centered? If you really want an answer to this question, talk to the youngsters themselves. Ask them to explain how they choose their books for pleasure, how they know when a draft is finished and how the classroom operates. If they can explain the program nearly as well as the teacher, you're probably in a whole language classroom.

REFLECTIONS

As your visit progressed, you may have found answers to many of your questions — only to discover that even more popped into your head. Make note of them as well as the context in which they arose so they can be discussed in the debriefing. Knowing the context will help the teacher provide a specific response. For example, during shared reading, you may have wondered why children's predictions about the story were praised even when they were inaccurate or why some students received more help than others with editing writing drafts.

After the children have left for the day, share your questions with the teacher. You may also want to find out more about some of the centers or materials used during the day. Ask the teacher to suggest sources of information about literature study groups or process writing and to recommend strategies for getting a whole language program started.

When you get home, try to list five things you learned about whole language and five questions you still want answered. Think about the classroom you observed. What aspects of the program were most familiar? Which were unclear or completely unfamiliar? These are the areas where professional reading is needed. The logical starting place is your own questions.

At this time, you may decide to visit another whole language classroom to obtain more ideas and see more materials. Before you schedule this, reflect on today's visit and digest the information you gathered. Do some additional reading and thinking. Jot down some ideas about things you'd like to see the teacher demonstrate. Then locate your list of whole language teachers and make new contacts. Your next visit should expand on many of the ideas you picked up.

. . . .

WHET YOUR APPETITE

So you like what you've found out so far and want to give whole language a try. Relax. You don't need to jump in all at once. You can start to get your toes wet by gradually incorporating some easily managed practices into your classroom. Implementing just one of the suggestions that follow will set you on the path towards becoming a whole language teacher. Don't expect instant results. Choose one idea and stay with it until you're comfortable. If you're not sure that you're doing things "right," check with another whole language teacher in your school or do some more reading.

Modify the Basal Reading Program

If you decide to ease into whole language by using basal readers and maintaining your reading groups, start by assessing your current program. What basal are you using? How many reading groups have you set up? How many different basal levels are they using? Will the administration allow you to modify basal lessons? Can you make changes in the workbook and skills lessons that will be acceptable to your principal?

You'll need the support of a reading teacher and your principal to get started, so it's important to know the answers to these questions before making changes. Because not all the following suggestions will meet your needs, do only as much as you feel comfortable with. You don't need to become a whole language teacher overnight!

You might try starting with only one of your reading groups. If you select the "top" group, containing the best readers in the class, they'll probably adjust easily to a change in classroom routine. It should be obvious that they don't need to complete the skill-and-drill sheets that accompany basal readers and they will likely welcome a chance to read "real" books of their own choosing.

On the other hand, less able readers will also be delighted to abandon skill-and-drill exercises in favor of reading "real" books. Contrary to belief, isolated skill-and-drill practice does little to improve reading skills. Like most skills, reading improves with practice, the kind of practice that comes from reading stories and articles.

Regardless of which group you select, the changes you make will require the children to engage in some of the cooperative learning activities and independent tasks that are the hallmark of whole language classrooms. Let the children know that they will be helping you learn about some new approaches to reading and writing. You'll need their feedback as you try out whole language activities and, if you approach the experiment cooperatively, you and the students will become partners in the project.

Once you've selected the group or groups, take a good look at your basal. Several components of traditional basal reader lessons can be safely omitted or modified during direct instruction:

— Teaching guides for basals often include lists of words to be introduced before reading a story. Rather than doing this, try incorporating the teaching of these words as the need arises in the context of the story. Don't misunderstand. Teaching vocabulary is important. But you needn't adhere strictly to the stated guidelines for pre-teaching words. You're the one who knows the children in your classroom and you can do the best job of selecting words for pre-teaching.
— Read the stories in the basal. Decide which are likely to interest and appeal to students, which contain useful information and which support social studies and science curricula. Eliminate those that may be difficult for children to follow or understand as well as those that are simply boring.

— Look at the questions ostensibly designed to guide the children's reading of the stories. If you read them carefully, you'll probably notice that, in fact, they often interfere with the flow of the story and fragment the story line. Ask yourself if they can be incorporated into broader, open-ended instructions and questions like, "Tell me about the story so far." "What have you learned about ____?" "Why do you think _____?" "What do you think will happen now?"

— Eliminate lessons that isolate and fragment skills. Skills should be taught in the context of the story as the need arises. Don't teach them on the chance that it might be good for the children. Remember, most children will use essential skills even if they are never taught directly.

— You'll probably find the enrichment activities suggested at the end of each lesson far more useful than the recommended skills lessons. Enrichment suggestions often make excellent whole class or independent activities. Be sure to read the suggestions for additional books that can be read to students and that students can read themselves. These bibliographies will help you become acquainted with the literature children enjoy at the grade level you're teaching. Enrichment suggestions often tie in with social studies and science curricula and can become an important teaching resource.

— Ask yourself if the workbook pages or ditto packets that accompany the basals are likely to help children understand the story. Because these often amount to little more than "busy work" that does nothing to foster comprehension, they should be avoided.

As you move towards whole language, then, you can continue to use stories in the basal. Be selective, however. Don't use every story. Read only those that fit in with the students' interests, classroom themes or authors you are studying. Eliminate those that are boring, difficult to understand or beyond the scope of students' experiential background.

ETR Lessons

Once most of the directed reading activities set out in the basal teaching guide are eliminated, you may find yourself asking just how reading and writing are to be taught. The experience-text-relationship — ETR — format described by Jana Mason and Kathryn Au in *Reading Instruction for Today* provides an excellent model that can be applied to stories from basals.

Advance planning is required, however. Begin by reading the story yourself and deciding on the central theme, main idea or major points to be highlighted. Develop a plan for introducing the story that will help children relate it to their own experiences. Then, keeping in mind the children's needs, interests and abilities, plan when you will stop during the reading to discuss the story. For example, primary-grade children might stop for discussion every couple of pages while more advanced readers might stop only once or even read the entire story right through.

The E — or experience — phase of this model calls on the teacher to introduce the story by initiating a discussion of experiences relating to the topic or theme. Ask the children to predict what they think might happen in the story, then direct them to read the text to find out what's in the story.

During the T — or text — phase, discuss the story with the children. Rather than conducting a factual question-and-answer session, encourage them to talk about what they read and their reactions. The discussion can include a check of their predictions. "Did you think this would happen?" "How do you feel about that?" "What do you think will happen next?" Use open-ended questions like these to encourage children to become involved with the story.

The R — or relationship — phase requires teachers to help youngsters connect what occurred in the story to their own experiences. This bridge between what actually happened and the students' perceptions of what should or might have happened is built by discussing and checking the story content against the children's predictions.

ETR lessons include opportunities for children to engage in independent activities relating to the story, such as working on appropriate workbook pages, completing teacher-created comprehension exercises, making visual maps of the story, drawing pictures to represent the story, reading the unabridged version of the story and comparing it to the basal version, and writing summaries, a new ending, character sketches and so on.

Though ETR lessons allow you to provide direct instruction and monitor the children's progress carefully, you're not restricted to teaching words the children already know or asking questions whose answers are readily evident. Instead, you tap the students' background knowledge, encourage them to predict what will occur next, listen to their comments and summaries and provide immediate clarification and opportunities to extend the information.

Flexible Groups

Once you've modified your basal lessons, you may be ready to try more whole language strategies. A flexible grouping plan that dispenses with the traditional ability-based high, middle and low reading groups can be your next step. This involves inviting children to form groups according to their interests or their work on special projects. These may focus on themes under study, authors, literary genres and special needs of individuals. As good readers work with less able readers, cooperative learning is stressed and all the children have an opportunity to contribute in their own way.

To begin, you might take another look at your existing resources, namely the basals. For example, if you decide to start with a theme, scan the major headings in the table of contents to find something suitable. Most basals are divided into sections based on common themes such as fairy tales, pets, wild animals, family trips, extinct species and so on.

From a number of basals, select stories that fit your theme. Remember, even if the reading levels are different, you can still use the stories. If interest is high and your instruction supportive, less able readers will still be able to understand stories in more advanced readers.

Examine the enrichment section of your basal for ideas for extending children's thinking about the topic and for encouraging independent work such as research, writing and art. Invite all the children to participate in the extension activities for this will help everyone feel involved in the topic, generating interest in and ownership of their work. Don't worry about the time it takes or the fact that they're not forging ahead to complete another story. Other more important things are happening.

Shared Reading

Rather than modifying your basal reading program, you may prefer to introduce whole language to your classroom by inviting the entire class to join in the shared reading of a big book.

Big books are picture books selected for enlargement because they possess special qualities that contribute to their predictability. These may include a one-to-one match between the text and illustrations, readily recognizable rhyme and rhythm patterns, familiar concepts or story lines, cumulative language or story patterns and repetitive language.

A shared reading approach is particularly appropriate for big book stories. As you talk about the book and read and reread the story with the children, they'll learn to make predictions about, discuss, question and anticipate events. They'll become comfortable chiming in and reading repetitive lines along with you. As they do so, they'll take their first step towards becoming independent readers.

Teaching strategies used during shared reading sessions will vary according to the title selected. For example, some stories invite children to make predictions before seeing a new page while others are so rich in repetitive language patterns that the children will naturally read along with you. The content of the book will define your approach to the session.

Shared reading helps children become readers naturally and joyously as they discover that reading is fun. For your part, you'll probably find yourself individualizing instruction and teaching to the children's strengths within the setting of the entire group. For example, you'll know when Mark has mastered the repetitive pattern and can read it aloud as you point to it or that Jack has a great idea about what will happen on the next page. With this approach, all the children can be "stars."

If you make the big book and standard-sized copies of the same title accessible to the children, they can reread the story on their own or with a buddy, helping each other with words, phrases and repetitive patterns. If the book isn't read word-for-word, it really doesn't matter because, as the children help each other, they are engaging in cooperative learning and imitating the behavior you have modeled.

Individualize Instruction

To accommodate differences in children's interests and reading abilities, whole language teachers help them select literacy activities that optimize their enthusiasm while promoting their reading and writing development. For example, if you have grouped the children according to interest rather than ability, not everyone will be able to participate at the same level. Some will excel in reading, some will be able to read only limited portions of stories and some will have to listen to stories rather than read them alone. By individualizing instruction, however, through activities such as response logs, sustained silent reading, buddy reading and contracts, everyone in the group can participate actively.

RESPONSE LOGS

Written response logs help the teacher keep abreast of the children's participation and involvement in literacy activities. Logs will vary in complexity and thoroughness. As the children respond, orally and in writing, to activities in which they've participated, you'll be able to follow up the written entries with questions and discussions.

At first, you may be discouraged because the children aren't writing as much as you think they should. Be patient. Read the response logs and ask them to explain a statement by writing some descriptive words, to clarify by suggesting an alternative interpretation, or to expand an idea by writing more detail.

SUSTAINED SILENT READING

Most whole language teachers include SSR (sustained silent reading) in their instructional sequences. Here, students select a favorite book to read or browse through. This time set aside for uninterrupted reading is their personal reading time. Everybody, including the teacher, reads a book or magazine of their choice. The rules of SSR are strict in that this period is not to be interrupted. This is not the time to catch up on attendance, lunch money, book orders and so on because, as you read your own book, you're modeling reading and demonstrating that recreational reading is important.

BUDDY READING

Buddy reading is just what the name suggests. In pairs, the children practice reading, taking turns being the reader and the listener-helper. Pairs can take many forms. Though it isn't uncommon to match a good reader with one who is less able, children of equal ability can also be paired. You might let the students select their own partners as long as they are compatible and able to work cooperatively. Buddy reading allows quite a bit of practice to occur without direct teacher intervention. It may be helpful if you model the roles of both the reader and the listener-helper for the children, showing them how they can support each other's efforts.

CONTRACTS

Some children work best when they have a pre-set schedule to follow or when they have participated in setting their own learning goals. Daily, weekly, bi-weekly or monthly contracts can be drawn up for those who prefer to work this way. The contract can spell out such things as the number of pages to be read and the kinds of responses required when engaging in reading and writing activities.

At the end of the pre-set period, the completed work is reviewed by the teacher and student and, together, they decide whether the contract has been completed.

Create a Literate Environment

Whole language classrooms are rich in printed materials and are structured to provide lots of opportunities for students to engage in purposeful reading and writing activities. The literacy program should capitalize on children's curiosity and natural enthusiasm, use natural texts and provide plenty of activities designed to encourage youngsters to apply their learning.

The physical environment of the classroom is an extension of the whole language teacher's philosophy and enhances his ability to accomplish instructional goals. Library centers, writing centers, message boards and working bulletin boards all help create a print-rich environment.

In an article in *The Reading Teacher*, Leslie Morrow indicated that well-designed library centers promote literacy development while poorly organized centers can end up virtually ignored by students. And in her book, *Literacy Development in the Early Years*, she identified several features that differentiate successful and unsuccessful library centers.

The library center should be a visually appealing focus of the classroom, attractively decorated with, for example, child-created posters that encourage reading or dust jackets from favorite books. It often helps if it is set off on two or three sides with bookshelves, walls, etc. and, if possible, it should be large enough to accommodate five or six children. To ensure that children are comfortable while they read, furniture such as a rocking chair, throw pillows or a sofa might be placed in the center.

The materials in the library center should encourage students to read and react to literature. Books representing a range of genres at a variety of reading levels, as well as magazines and newspapers, should be available. For primary students, big books as well as an easel and a pointer might be accessible.

In *Children's Literature in the Elementary School*, Charlotte Huck, Susan Helpler and Janet Hickman recommend that the center contain five to eight titles per student. The supply of books, which may come from school or public libraries, flea markets and donations from parents, should be changed frequently and displayed enticingly. For younger children, books might be color-coded and arranged according to subject or type. For example, yellow dots might indicate animal stories and so on. Books for older students might be categorized according to genres, themes or authors depending on your literacy goals and objectives.

Books you wish to draw attention to might be displayed separately. These displays should be changed regularly to include titles that reflect themes currently under study or that tie in with content subjects.

Library centers should also be stocked with materials that will encourage students to retell and create new versions of their favorite stories. Felt and magnetic boards, puppets and puppet theaters, prop boxes and roll-top movie boxes all motivate students to retell stories. Whereas primary students will need these materials made for them, children in the intermediate grades will enjoy creating their own materials for retelling and re-enacting stories.

Library centers in primary classrooms should also engage students in other literacy learning activities. Materials such as magnetic letters, alphabet cards, jigsaw sight word puzzles, sound-sorting activities and story sequence cards help students acquire knowledge of sight words and phonetic generalizations incidentally.

If desired, a table for listening and viewing might be placed in the library center. A tape recorder with multiple headphones allows students to listen to commercially produced tapes, class-produced readings of big books and individual or group readings of self-authored texts. An automatic filmstrip projector and small viewing screen also invites them to view filmstrips.

A library center is an integral component of whole language classrooms. Provide students with ample time to use the center and incorporate it into reading lessons as much as possible. Remember, if you treat the library center as separate from reading lessons, the children will develop the same perceptions.

WRITING CENTER

An oasis for young authors, the writing center should be visually appealing and contain a wealth of writing tools, writing motivaters and reference aids. It should be located near the library center so that books and props found there will stimulate children to write their own stories.

Ideally, the writing center, which may also include computer equipment, should be stocked with materials like staples, scissors and paper for making books, a chalkboard, dictionaries, thesauruses, atlases, sample letters and so on to provide models for the children's own writing, editor's marks for reference, story starter cards, wordless books where the children can fill in the story, old magazines and catalogues for cutting up, alphabet models and so on.

The writing center should be designed to foster independent as well as collaborative work. A table with four chairs or four desks pushed together is appropriate. Folding screens are helpful when children desire privacy. Some students may wish to stretch out and write on the carpet in the library center and should be allowed to do so.

Each child should have a personal writing folder for storing written work. If all work is dated, improvements over the course of the year can be tracked. The folder should contain current projects, while other works are stored in a cumulative file that both the child and teacher have access to.

Introduce new writing motivaters periodically to keep the center exciting and, once it is in place, be sure to provide many opportunities for students to use it. Remember, children learn to write by writing and the writing center encourages engagement in purposeful writing activities.

MESSAGE BOARD

Because children read and write as they send messages to and receive them from the teacher, their parents and each other, a message board is one way of encouraging them to engage in meaningful literacy activities.

Creating a message board is relatively easy. Just select a bulletin board that is accessible to everyone and cover it with colored construction paper, wrapping paper or some other attractive material. Label it with colorful letters. Place writing paper, envelopes, an assortment of writing tools and thumbtacks on a table or desk nearby.

Introduce the message board by sending the first message yourself. This might be an announcement to the entire class, a message to a particular student or an invitation to parents. Once the children discover the message, encourage them to send their own messages to one another and to you. These can be posted openly or placed in envelopes. It's a good idea to insist that all messages be signed and, to keep the board current, dated.

The teacher plays in integral role in keeping the board alive by varying the kinds of messages displayed. The board can be used as a place to sign up for classroom activities, praise student work, share stories, keep track of classroom events, exchange letters with members of another class and so on.

In whole language classrooms, the children's own creations form an important part of the print-rich environment and working bulletin boards acknowledge this. While some working bulletin boards may be initiated by the teacher, it's a good idea to encourage the children to take over responsibility for them.

If the children have, for example, written their own version of a big book story, they might divide into groups to illustrate the pages. Once completed, these can be displayed on the working bulletin board.

Many literature extension activities, such as collages, cooperative paintings and photographic essays, make excellent working bulletin boards. As they create the boards, invite the children to experiment with a variety of materials — fabrics, different types of paints, crayons, chalks, newspapers, tagboard and so on.

Working bulletin boards can also include calendars that are updated daily, poetry boards that consist of a piece of poetry accompanied by the students' artistic interpretations, message boards as previously described, and bulletin boards that entice students to increase their vocabulary or engage in activities that reinforce other areas of the curriculum. It won't be long before the children begin to come up with their own ideas. Creating working bulletin boards encourages collaboration and a sense of ownership of classroom activities, important characteristics of child-centered classrooms.

. . . .

EXPLORE CHILDREN'S LITERATURE

Children's literature is central to the whole language approach. While strategies, environments and schedules may vary from teacher to teacher, good literature is always the focus of whole language classrooms. By providing children with a multitude of vicarious experiences, literature increases background knowledge, introduces new friends, presents new challenges and engages children in new adventures. As they enter new worlds and empathize with the characters they meet there, children learn more about themselves and the human condition.

The primary goals of a good literature program include developing a love of reading, an interest in books and life-long reading and writing habits. An appreciation of genres, an understanding of literary elements and increased background knowledge are natural by-products of this approach.

Though planning a literature-based program is time-consuming, the rewards are many. Begin slowly. Try a themed unit or an author study, extend the basal lessons you've already modified with further related readings or read aloud to your students. Once you enter the world of children's literature, there will be no turning back.

Getting Started

Whole language teachers continually update their knowledge of children's literature. This includes expanding their familiarity with literary genres, favorite authors, award-winning works, criteria for selecting children's books and ideas for presenting literature to youngsters. An awareness of children's interests and the importance of developing motivating instructional practices is also necessary. Many resources are available to help novice whole language teacher discover children's literature.

LITERARY GENRES

Whole language classrooms are rich in literature because teachers know that children read more when books are readily accessible in library centers that contain a sampling of high-quality titles representing a variety of genres.

Although some students may become stuck reading books in a single genre, a talented teacher can help them develop an appreciation for other literary forms. Tastes in reading can be broadened when a teacher creates a literate environment in which books are easily located, models a love of reading, reads aloud to students, reads silently during sustained silent reading time and integrates literature across the curriculum. A working knowledge of children's literature and organizational schemes for sharing literature will help create a literate environment.

LOCATING CHILDREN'S LITERATURE

Titles such as *Through the Eyes of a Child: An Introduction to Children's Literature, Children and Books* and *Children's Literature in the Elementary School* are excellent guides to choosing children's books. Organized according to genre with a list of recommended titles and authors in each category, they also cite Caldecott and Newbery award-winners.

Once you're familiar with genres, bibliographies, which usually contain cross-referenced subject, author and title indexes, become more meaningful. *Children's Books in Print,* which categorizes more than 45,000 titles, and Carolyn and John Lima's *A to Zoo: Subject Access to Children's Picture Books,* which lists about 4,500 titles, are massive in scope. Other bibliographies, though not as comprehensive, provide useful annotated entries. These include such titles as John Gillespie and Christine Gilbert's *Best Books for Children: Preschool through the Middle Grades,* Michele Landsberg's *Reading for the Love of It,* Zena Sutherland's *The Best in Children's Books* and

George Wilson and Joyce Moss's *Books for Children to Read Alone: A Guide for Parents and Librarians.*

While these bibliographies are general in scope, others pertain to specific subject areas. Titles such as Vandelia VanMeter's *American History for Children and Young Adults: An Annotated Bibliography* are invaluable resources for teachers interested in integrating literature across the curriculum. Many bibliographies focus on literature dealing with sensitive issues, such as divorce, death and handicaps. *The Bookfinder: A Guide to Children's Literature about the Needs and Problems of Youth Aged 2-15* (Vol. 40) by Sharon Dreyer, *Children's Literature: An Issues Approach* (2nd Ed.) by Masha Rudman and *Growing Pains: Helping Children Deal with Everyday Problems through Reading* by Maureen Cuddigan and Mary Hanson are all helpful.

Literary journals are also excellent resources for locating recently published children's books. For example, *The School Library Journal, Booklist, Language Arts, The Reading Teacher* and the *Horn Book* contain book reviews. Every October, *The Reading Teacher* publishes "Children's Choices," an annotated list of books selected by youngsters across the United States. This is followed in November by "Teachers' Choices," an annotated list of teachers' favorites.

Many award-granting agencies publish lists of the books that have won over the years. For a complete list of international awards, consult *Children's Books: Awards and Prizes,* published by the Children's Book Council.

In addition to locating quality children's books, whole language teachers must be familiar with the works themselves so they can start orchestrating that perfect match between child and book.

SELECTING MATERIALS TO READ ALOUD

When choosing read-aloud materials, it's important that *you* like the selection. You're more likely to elicit an emotional response from your audience if you're involved with the story yourself. The literary tastes of children and adults aren't necessarily different. If a book doesn't hold your interest, there's a good chance children will feel the same way.

It's also critical that the selection be well-written. Books with vivid characterization, interesting dialogue and a well-paced storyline that emphasizes action rather than description make good read-aloud selections. Read-alouds need to capture student interest from the outset. In *The New Read-Aloud Handbook,* Jim Trelease says, "Books and readers are very much like fishing rods and fish. Since the object of every good book is to catch readers, it should come equipped with a hook, a piece of the story's framework that grabs the reader and holds them through all 24 or 224 pages. There must be just the right amount of tension in the story line: it must be loose enough to kindle the reader's imagination; yet tight enough to keep the reader's constant attention."

When selecting picture books for read-alouds, look for illustrations that provide a one-to-one match with the text and that capture the essence of or expand the story. They should also be large enough for all the children to see them easily.

Selecting chapter books presents different challenges, for the children's interest must be maintained from day to day as the reading continues. Good read-aloud chapter books have natural stopping points that leave listeners wanting more.

Finally, keep your listeners in mind. Their ages, interests, past experiences and attention spans will play a crucial role in defining your choices. Your school librarian can help you make appropriate selections. Resources such as *The New Read-Aloud Handbook* and Margaret Kimmel and Elizabeth Segel's *For Reading Out Loud: A Guide to Sharing Books with Children* are also helpful.

SELECTING BOOKS FOR INDEPENDENT READING

Because the books children select for recreational reading often reflect their personal interests, a well-developed classroom library should contain a wide variety of books representing all literary genres. Classroom library selections should also take into account the range of children's reading abilities as well as curricular needs. There should be a balance between the classics and more recent titles. The references mentioned earlier will help you put together an appropriate mix.

To draw children's attention to the books, teachers can set up appealing displays around a particular topic or theme, content subject, literary genre or sensitive issue that is currently being discussed. Other displays might focus on book award recipients or favorite authors. The children themselves can become involved in the selection process by compiling a list of their own "Children's Choices," locating them in the school or public library and sharing them with the class.

While self-selection is an important element of independent reading programs, teachers play a major role in making titles available and appealing to young readers.

Teaching Strategies

To make literature an integral and appealing part of the curriculum, whole language teachers use a variety of organizational patterns and techniques. Some, such as ETR lessons, flexible groups and shared reading have been mentioned earlier. As you become comfortable with children's literature, you may find yourself ready to begin experimenting with bibliotherapy, author studies and themed units.

BIBLIOTHERAPY

Bibliotherapy is defined in *A Dictionary of Reading and Related Terms* as "the use of selected writings to help the reader grow in self awareness and/or solve personal problems." In classrooms, bibliotherapy has been used to help students relate to others, appreciate problems common to children and adults everywhere and deal with their doubts and fears. Bibliotherapy can be tailored to meet the needs of individual children or influence the attitudes of an entire class.

The healing powers of literature have long been recognized by the medical profession. Although the therapeutic value of books and stories was documented as early as the 1920s, it wasn't until the 1940s that this notion was taken beyond the medical profession and adopted by teachers and librarians. Today, the surge of realistic fiction on the market presents renewed opportunities for teachers interested in helping children increase their understanding of themselves and others through books.

In an article in *Language Arts*, Cheryl Corman says that bibliotherapy takes readers through the following steps:

— Initially, the reader identifies and forms a bond with a story character. The reader begins to "live the other's life."

- Once this identification is established, a catharsis takes place. As the character works through a problem, the reader experiences an emotional release.
- As the reader realizes that the character's actions or attitudes apply to real-life situations, a new perspective on how she or he might handle a similar experience is gained.

Children will not experience these stages unless teachers select books in which the characters, content and situations are believable. Initially, teachers need to acquaint themselves with children's books dealing with sensitive issues. Resources such as those mentioned earlier make good starting places. If teachers want to introduce the texts to the entire class, the book might be read aloud. If this is the case, the guidelines for selecting read-alouds should be followed.

In *Children's Literature: An Issues Approach,* Masha Rudman suggests that the likelihood of success is enhanced if the books are presented informally. Never should a child be forced to read a selection, nor should books be prescribed for particular students. Rather, lure youngsters into reading by displaying books related to a sensitive issue or theme, posting titles in the library center and making suggestions during reading and writing conferences. Once a selection has been read, provide opportunities for discussion, extension activities and more reading on the same topic. Remember, teachers are not therapists. There is no guarantee that a book will influence a particular child or that the influence will be in the desired direction. Bibliotherapy works best with students who are not severely maladjusted. Nevertheless, literature is a powerful tool for self-discovery and teachers play a crucial role in bringing books and children together.

AUTHOR STUDIES

Author studies help familiarize children with literature. If they are to become authors in their own right, it is important for them to be familiar with what authors do. As they discover the writing techniques and styles of their favorite authors, they will begin doing what Frank Smith calls reading like writers.

In the primary grades, examining the works of author-illustrators provides children with opportunities to compare and contrast pictures as well as story elements. In the intermediate grades, authors who write stories with wide appeal that are age and interest appropriate should be selected. You might begin by introducing other works by the author of a favorite basal reader selection or a student's recreational reading choice. You can also select authors whose names appear on book award lists.

Begin by reading aloud one of the author's books. After the reading, discuss story elements such as characterization, setting, plot and theme, as well as writing style and technique. Then read aloud a second book and invite students to compare the two. In addition to comparing story elements, they might look for similarities and differences in samplings of the words used in the selections, the lessons the author was trying to teach and so on. At this point, the teacher may suggest other titles by the same author. These might be read and discussed individually or in groups and shared with the class.

Once several selections have been read, students can begin brainstorming what they feel they know about the author. What kind of a person do they feel the author is? What experiences do they feel the author might have had? Invite them to arrange the author's works chronologically and speculate about changes in his or her life. At this point, students may be ready to start compiling biographical information. Resources such as *Something about the Author: Facts and Pictures about Contemporary Authors and Illustrators of Books for Young People* or *The Sixth Book of Junior Authors and Illustrators* provide useful information. A committee of students might be interested in organizing the information acquired and presenting it to the class. The author study could culminate with a "Celebrate the Author" day.

THEMES

Themed units are another way of organizing curriculum around children's books. Literary works are selected to focus on a particular topic such as a science concept, a historical period or a literary genre. Author studies and readings about sensitive issues also qualify as themed units. An approach like this provides opportunities for students to collaborate as they work on group projects spanning the curriculum.

According to Christine Pappas, Barbara Kiefer and Linda Levstik in *An Integrated Language Perspective in the Elementary School: Theory in Action*, certain steps are necessary in planning a thematic unit. The theme should be common to a number of subject areas. For example, a unit on magic might spark a study of camouflage, which exemplifies the magic of nature. It might also touch on the magic of numbers, engaging students in "mind-reading" tricks with mathematical explanations. Students can research the history of magic, writing reports about famous magicians. And, as they attempt to perform their own magic tricks, they'll learn the importance of following written directions. They might also explore traditional tales with magical elements and respond to their readings through various creative extension activities.

Once you've selected a topic, locate the resources that will be used and plan activities to provide students with opportunities for purposeful listening, speaking, reading and writing. There should be ample opportunity for whole group, small group and individual projects. While the teacher will plan many of the activities at first, once the unit is under way, students may wish to pursue their own projects and ideas.

When the unit is introduced, try to motivate the children by reading aloud an interesting story or suggesting a hands-on activity. Once the topic has been introduced, follow up with whole class, small group and individual activities. Provide a variety of projects to choose from. Identify your expectations, negotiate agreements with individuals and devise a record-keeping system to log students' progress. They should have an opportunity to share their projects with one another.

Planning a thematic unit can seem like an overwhelming task at first. Many of the resources listed in the bibliography contain prototypes of themed units which you can adapt to satisfy your needs. Remember, the transition to a whole language classroom is a journey that takes place over time, not a race to a predetermined finish line. Dare to experiment with themed units and be patient with yourself and the students until everyone feels comfortable.

. . . .

WATCH LEARNING HAPPEN

Evaluation is a critically important element of any classroom program. Parents and teachers want to know what was learned and how learning occurred and children, too, need feedback about their progress.

In traditional programs, assessment involves testing children's mastery of skills or information — can they name the letters of the alphabet, for example, or correctly identify the sounds represented by the letters? In general, children are evaluated according to how well their performance stacks up against that of other students at the same grade level. In many cases, this involves standardized tests. Although this kind of testing may have value in some instances, it is not the primary yardstick used to measure learning in whole language classrooms.

Assessment in whole language programs uses measures that affirm the learning experiences that have occurred in the classroom. It's rooted in the understanding that no two children are alike. They come from different cultural and experiential backgrounds, enter classrooms at different developmental stages and operate at different learning rates and with different styles.

Whole language teachers understand that they really are in charge of their classrooms and must actively guide and assess the children's learning experiences all day long. They don't rely on commercially produced reproducibles to keep the children busy or teach to the questions likely to appear on a published test. All assessment requires teachers to develop a mental and physical framework for collecting, interpreting and evaluating data. In whole language classrooms, where assessment practices are geared to instructional goals, teaching and evaluation often occur at the same time, requiring the teacher to take a mental step back to give full attention to both instruction and evaluation.

Your evaluation procedures need not be completely in place before you start your whole language journey. As your knowledge of literacy development expands, you'll naturally begin to use some whole language assessment techniques. The measures you choose will take into account the children's developmental stages, their level of literacy development and their cultural backgrounds as well as your intended purposes. Just as children become literate by engaging in reading and writing activities, you'll become effective at evaluating children's learning by engaging in child-centered assessment procedures.

Start slowly at first by incorporating one or two of the following suggestions. As you become comfortable with one technique, try another. Don't attempt to do everything at once. Make sure you're satisfied with the information you're getting from one strategy before you try a new idea.

Unstructured Evaluation Measures

Many of the assessment procedures used in whole language classrooms are informal and unstructured. These include reviewing children's past records, talking with previous teachers, observing, discussing with the children, notetaking and keeping journals and portfolio records.

PREVIOUS RECORDS

Get to know the children by reviewing their school records and talking to the previous year's teacher. Doing this need not compromise your judgment and will likely prove helpful. You'll find out about things like the family structure, allergies, attendance patterns, interests, fears, major illnesses and behavior. Knowing that certain patterns are likely to surface in a given situation will help you plan more effectively.

If your school uses standardized tests, check the children's scores. Though you may disagree with standardized tests and prefer informal evaluation techniques, don't ignore this information if it's available. You can learn some very useful things from test records. For example, has a child made progress each year? How much progress? Has there been a year when little progress occurred? Use records to establish a broad perspective on the children's performance. Be careful to verify items you question and avoid gearing your own expectations to the scores.

Percentile rank results are often the most useful and easily understood of the variety of test data available to teachers. For easy reference, make a thumbnail profile of essential data for each child. It might look like this:

Mary's Standardized Test Scores

Grade	Percentile Rdg Vocab	Percentile Rdg Comp	Percentile Wd Recog	Days Attended
1	72	65	75	167
2	75	67	76	172
3	45	48	60	100
4	60	67	64	170

This information should tell you that this child, Mary, usually performs as well as or better than 60 to 75 percent of the children at her grade level. But look at her ranking in the third grade when her percentile scores dropped considerably. Her attendance also dropped that year. We can assume that something happened to prevent her from attending school, perhaps a long illness, surgery or a serious family problem. Her ranking in grade four indicates that she may be returning to her earlier form. Be careful not to draw too many conclusions, however. Talk to other teachers and find out if your interpretations are correct. Previous records provide you with baseline information that should be checked against other sources such as last year's teacher and your own observations.

INFORMAL OBSERVATION

Data compiled from observations become part of an assessment program when you systematically listen to, watch and talk to the children. Begin by noting and recording behaviors related to the goals of your classroom. For example, the first time David points to words as he reads suggests that he is beginning to understand the concept of word boundaries. The first time Susie reads the big book to her peers suggests that she understands that print carries a message that can be shared. And when Molly expresses an interest in reading books about horses, the teacher has learned something about her likes.

Teachers often need practice before they feel comfortable recording observational data. Begin by taking a look at the children in your classroom and thinking about what you're seeing and hearing. Identify a few behaviors that you'd like to observe. For example, you might decide to start by watching children's facial expressions and body movements as they read. In just a few minutes, you'll note that Latoya sits up very straight in her chair, points to words with her finger and smiles every so often as she reads an amusing line. On the other hand, Jake is a wiggler. How can he remember what he reads? His feet are in constant motion, he hardly glances at the page and yet he can tell you all about the story. Practice recording the observed behaviors in a such a way that you'll understand what you've written later.

You may be wondering how, with a class of 25 children, you'll find time to keep observational records. It's important to remember that you don't have to record observations about every child every day. Record only noteworthy information indicating that a change in a child's literacy acquisition is occurring or has occurred. Otherwise, you'll have page after page of useless information about various children and you'll probably decide that this method isn't for you.

Note how children approach assignments and interact with their peers and with you. Does their behavior during independent activities differ from the way they act during teacher-directed instruction? For example, John protests, "Oh no!! Not another story to write!" But then he picks up his pencil and writes a good story about his trip to Disneyworld. Jennifer, on the other hand, doesn't say word when she's given a writing assignment. She takes out her folder and looks at it for 30 minutes but doesn't write. Behaviors like these have always been observed by teachers. Now it's important to raise your awareness and include them in your notes.

Make your observations informally at first. Periodically, ask yourself what you've learned about the students. Pretend you're going to report to parents, a placement committee, the principal or other teachers. What will you say? What notes will you need to refresh your memory?

INFORMAL DISCUSSIONS WITH CHILDREN

The best way to get to know children, to find out what they're thinking about or how they're doing with assignments is simply to talk to them and to ask. Do this as the opportunity arises or set aside a specific time to talk to particular individuals or small groups. Inquire about the books they're reading, the stories they're writing, the pictures they're drawing and how they feel about particular learning situations, themselves as learners and their reading and writing progress.

The need for help and instructional intervention will surface during your talk and discussion time. For example, Mrs. Beeler is circulating around her second-grade classroom. Stopping at Margie's desk, she sees that Margie has already drawn a picture but hasn't written anything. Mrs. Beeler says something like, "That's a nice picture. Do you want to write about it?" When Margie expresses the frustration she is experiencing over getting her thoughts down on paper, Mrs. Beeler says, "Well, try to say your idea." When Margie does so, she says, "Great! Now write that on your paper," then moves on to Sam who has just put down his book. She asks, "Why did you choose this book to read?" After he responds, she continues with questions and comments like, "What's your favorite part?" "Does that remind you of something special?" "I'd like to hear your favorite part."

When Mrs. Beeler meets the group that has just read *Charlotte's Web*, all the children have a chance to share their favorite parts. Jimmy, who seldom volunteers information, tells the group how sad he felt about Wilbur, the pig, when he was going to be sent to market. Mrs. Beeler hadn't realized how sensitive Jimmy really was until she heard him describe this reaction. Talk and discussion increases understanding and provides insights into the complex thinking of others. While the information gleaned is unstructured and difficult to report as so-called data, discussion times set the stage for understanding children in different school settings.

Information and data gathered from observations and discussions can be recorded in a looseleaf notebook, on index cards or on self-sticking notes that can be attached to the page set aside for each child. Regardless of the format you select, be sure that information about individual children is organized so that it can be readily located. Record the children's name, address, telephone number, birthdate and grade. Directly below this, include one or two sentences describing the child. This information is unique for each individual and will help you remember special qualities such as fears, interests and approaches to learning. Each entry should be dated and include a few sentences recording the children's learning milestones or special difficulties. You'll have to decide when to make entries, what information to record and how to use the information for planning instruction and reporting progress. A sample record using self-sticking notes is found in Appendix 2.

JOURNAL-KEEPING

Set aside a time every few days to write in your own journal, perhaps during sustained silent writing periods. You'll be surprised at how much information about the children will surface as you keep this running account of what's happening in your classroom. For example, Mrs. Davis, a first-grade teacher, wrote the following account.

"I was pleased with Mary today. She wouldn't even participate in the shared book lesson on Monday, but today, Thursday, she really knew the story and contributed more than the other children.

"Italo has me puzzled. I can't seem to find a way to help him pay attention. He looks all around the room and is in constant motion at his desk. He doesn't bother the other children but I don't think he's learning very much. I'll talk to the principal about him if he continues these behaviors.

"I need to find a better management system for Shawn. He surprised me when he pushed Jamie for no apparent reason today. He seems very angry. I think I'll talk to him tomorrow about this.

"Pamjit was wonderful today. After three months of scribble writing, she wrote her name and used alphabet letters to write her story. She was very proud of herself and I was very proud of her."

TAPED OBSERVATIONS

A small, hand-held tape recorder is a useful tool for recording observations when you don't have time to write. If you use a tape recorder, be sure to tell your students why you're talking into it and how you'll use your spoken notes. Some teachers have found that tape recorders intimidate children, inhibiting their responses. You might explain that this is your reminder of what happened during the day. Later, listen to the tape and transcribe important information into your journal or notebook. You'll be surprised at the amount of information that can be gleaned about the class as a whole, individual children and yourself.

PORTFOLIO ASSESSMENT

Maintaining a file folder for each child is a very efficient and practical way of monitoring progress. Periodically, add samples of the children's work in reading and writing. Portfolio assessment allows you to trace the children's growth as learners by examining their work from the beginning of the school year to the end. Be sure to collect samples of the same kinds of work. For example, samples of independent writing, writing done as a group project and expository and creative writing are needed. Summaries of books read, running records of familiar, current and unfamiliar books and reading, writing, speaking and listening checklists should also be included. Other information such as drawings, letters from the children or parents, records of your interviews with the children and an attitude inventory complete the folder.

You'll need to become adept at "reading" the information by interpreting the samples in terms of the changes you see. A sample record from one child's portfolio is shown in Appendix 3. You'll note that the teacher read the child's story and jotted down information gleaned from the sample. The child's work as well as the teacher's comments make this valuable data.

Structured Evaluation Measures

Structured measures, such as keeping checklists, running records, logs of books read and writing completed, writing samples and records of interviews with the children, provide specific quantitative information about certain learning tasks. Though each technique addresses a different aspect of assessment, you needn't use them all. Start with a procedure that matches your instructional purpose, that you feel comfortable using, and that provides the most reliable information.

CHECKLISTS

Though checklists are commonly used assessment procedures, they're like light switches — either on or off. They don't tell us anything about the quality of an event, only that it occurred. Nevertheless, they're convenient, flexible and easy for both teachers and children to maintain.

The first step in making up a checklist involves identifying essential literacy behaviors associated with particular age and grade level. This is often completed by a team of teachers of the same grade level who conduct a "task analysis" of expected learning behaviors to determine categories and criteria. Checklists should include specific information about these five categories of literacy development: listening, speaking, handwriting, reading and writing.

Requirements for marking the categories can be as simple as YES the learning has been acquired or NO it has not. More sophisticated checklists allow the degree of learning to be recorded. For example, the reading checklist in Appendix 4 includes four categories: never, sometimes, frequently and not observed. Checklists can be completed every few months and may replace traditional report cards. Parents can see the behaviors and skills children should be acquiring in relation to what they have acquired. See Appendixes 5 through 7 for sample checklists in writing, emergent writing, listening and speaking.

Checklists also help teachers develop guidelines for informal assessment. In fact, the formal checklist can set out the criteria on which informal assessment is based. Once the major learning concepts and behavior patterns are identified, it's easy to determine what to observe and record. Remember to evaluate in relation to your instructional goals, however. For example, if one of your purposes is to encourage children to enjoy reading, then you need to note behavior that reflects whether this goal has been achieved. Your notes and journal-keeping will provide the data that will help you mark the checklists.

RUNNING RECORDS

If you want to know how well children read, listen to them. Running records, which are a teacher's shorthand record of the miscues children make as they read aloud, provide a formal transcripts of reading sessions.

Marie Clay suggests that teachers use three types of passages for running records: a very familiar selection that has been shared several times, a selection that is currently being used for instruction and has been read only once or twice, and a selection that is new to the child. The criterion for selecting passages for running records, then, is the child's familiarity with the text. Genres and types of text, such as narrative and expository, should not be mixed when selecting passages.

You'll need acetate sheets to place over your copy of the readings so words can be marked as the child reads. You'll also need to familiarize yourself with the coding system used for marking. Because you'll need instruction, practice and guidance in scoring and interpreting the records, it's a good idea to ask the reading specialist for help at first. More detailed information can be found in Clay's book, *The Early Detection of Reading Difficulties.*

READING AND WRITING LOGS

Reading and writing logs are children's own records of the books they have read and the writing they have completed. The logs can be kept in a folder and stored in an appropriate area in the classroom. They have special value, for they encourage students to become involved in the process of planning and assessing their own learning.

Sample logs, as well as an alarm clock reading form, are contained in Appendix 8. The alarm clock reading form is particularly useful for monitoring progress through books selected for sustained silent reading or drop everything and read (DEAR) times.

The information in the children's logs is an important element of whole language assessment programs and should be reviewed periodically. Check the number of books read, the number of pages read, the writing drafts and the writing that has been completed. Evaluate what the children are reading and writing in relation to their reading and writing ability and grade level. This will help you set expectations for each child. For example, Mr. Bellmar looked at Melissa's reading log and found that she had read only 10 pages over the course of the week. He was concerned because she usually reads about twice that number. He reviewed the week's activities and recalled that there were two special assemblies and that Melissa was absent on Wednesday. This mental review explained the drop in her reading. If he hadn't found reasons for the decline, he would have discussed his concerns with Melissa. This kind of personal connection is one of the most positive features of whole language evaluation programs.

The writing log can also be used for periodic assessment of the progress of individual children. Examine the log for topics of interest, writing that has been completed, types of writing (e.g., narrative or expository), abandoned topics and partially completed work.

Note the patterns that appear. For example, Jake's log indicates that he has abandoned nine of the 10 topics in his folder. You conclude that he may need to develop strategies for pre-writing and brainstorming. Maybe he's starting his drafts before his ideas are developed well enough. Tara, on the other hand, has listed 15 topics that she's interested in writing about but hasn't begun to write any drafts. Her log suggests that she needs instruction in brainstorming about a specific topic. Peter's log indicates that he's written several drafts but hasn't yet revised, edited or published anything. You'll need to investigate whether he needs help to complete his drafts or whether he's a perfectionist who won't publish because he isn't satisfied with his writing. He may need some conference time as well as direct help.

Reading and writing logs help children establish assessment procedures for themselves as well as their own goals for reading and writing. Your reviews take only a few minutes yet they provide important information. If the reading and writing patterns are normal, intervention isn't necessary. If a change in the normal pattern is evident, however, it takes only a few minutes to investigate the problem.

Children's logs also reveal their interests. For example, Susie reads about dolls and horses while Sugith enjoys books about nature and detective stories. Information like this helps you select appropriate books for the classroom library. Children are pleased when their teacher remembers what kinds of books they like and finds just the right one for them. As you examine the children's choices of authors and genres, you'll also note changes in their reading levels. For example, Steve started his reading log in September with a very short, easy-to-read picture book but now, in December, he's reading longer chapter books more appropriate to his instructional level. These changes are noteworthy and should be shared with Steve and his parents as a marker of his growing maturity in reading. Meg's writing log listed horses as her only topic in September. Now she's writing about her antique doll collection and her family's trips.

Because logs provide teachers with both qualitative and quantitative information, children should be instructed in their use and provided with feedback about their reading, writing and record-keeping.

WRITING SAMPLES

Individual writing samples provide another important medium for evaluation in whole language classrooms. They are an effective yardstick of writing growth, for each individual's progress is measured against his or her initial performance, not the grade level standard. Some schools collect and save three writing samples over the course of every school year, gathering them at the beginning, middle and end. In addition to evaluating growth over the course of a single year, these samples effectively measure growth through the grades.

Within the classroom, teachers should periodically — about every six weeks — collect writing samples from the children. Try to collect examples of narrative and expository writing, including the drafts of each piece to see how children have revised ideas from draft to draft. If you teach conventions such as capitalization, paragraphing, friendly letters and so on, collect samples of work using these conventions. Read the writing samples and record important information. You'll use this information during conferences with parents and the children and when you need to report the child's progress to other school personnel.

Spelling usually develops because children want to learn to spell the words used in writing. Teachers must be careful not to overemphasize the importance of correct spelling, a practice that can inhibit the free expression of the writer. Better for children with something to say to feel free to say it rather than limit themselves to writing a litany of sentences containing only words they know how to spell.

INTERVIEWS

Interviews with the children are a straightforward way to learn about how they view reading and writing, classroom teaching procedures and strategies, and themselves as readers and writers. This is valuable information and interview records (see Appendixes 9 and 10) should be stored in assessment portfolios. Compare the children's responses to reading and writing to your own views. If their responses indicate that they don't see the classroom as a cooperative environment, you'll need to analyze your practices and procedures. Then observe individuals closely to see how they approach learning tasks. This will give you further insight into the differences that may exist between your perceptions of the classroom and the children's.

. . . .

BUILD A SUPPORT NETWORK

Now that your journey towards whole language is well under way, you may find that the reading you've done, the classroom visits you've made, the literacy activities you've tried in your own classroom and your experiences with evaluation procedures have sparked a desire to learn more. In addition, the children's successful responses to literature and writing are exciting and you may wish you could share them with others. At the same time, you'd like to benefit from the experiences of teachers who may have asked the same questions and experimented with the same answers as you. All these needs can be addressed through a whole language teachers' support group.

Teacher-initiated support groups function in many areas. Some are formed by supervisors who may have contacted interested teachers at in-service programs. These groups are intended to keep the excitement and momentum generated by the program going and to extend the topics as teachers try new strategies with their students. Other groups are created within a school as four or five teachers meet to share their successes and questions. Eventually, teachers from various grade levels and schools may be invited to join and share information. Membership usually grows through word-of-mouth as teachers discover their own need to participate.

Teachers are well aware of the difficulty involved in trying whole language on your own, especially when you're the only one in your school or district. It can be hard to keep going when there's no one to answer your questions or provide encouragement when you feel stuck. Thus, the purpose of the groups, regardless of their size, is to support each teacher as whole language strategies are implemented and to offer help as they evolve in response to the changing needs of the children.

If you wish to locate a teacher-support group in your area, contact the Whole Language Umbrella, which operates an information clearinghouse, or the Whole Language Special Interest Group of the International Reading Association. Addresses for both are listed in the bibliography.

If there is no teacher-support group in your area, you may have to start your own. Why not circulate fliers to neighboring schools, inviting interested teachers to join you in an informal discussion of whole language? Even if you receive only four or five inquiries, you have enough interest to justify starting a group. Choose a meeting time and place — a school, your home, a restaurant, a bar, a church or a teacher center — and get started.

Tips for Organizing Meetings

Without a clear focus for meetings, teacher-initiated support groups can wither and die as fast as they're formed. Most groups survey their members to develop a list of concerns that serve as discussion topics at future meetings. While many groups meet monthly, others schedule weekly meetings that members are free to attend depending on their interest in the topic. This means that valuable meeting time is designated for addressing the needs of the membership.

During its first year, one teacher support group, composed of 12 teachers, decided to focus on using literature instead of basal readers. Together they brainstormed to make a list of topics they felt would provide them with a variety of choices. Some of the topics were suggested by articles they had read, others by materials they had seen used in classrooms. Their final "wish list" included a demonstration of shared reading, ways to use predictable books for word recognition, patterned writing from predictable books, wordless books as sources for writing and storytelling, role-playing and puppetry, and storymapping strategies. Because the group is teacher-initiated, the choice and order of topics reflect the changing needs of the members.

Once a list of topics is decided on, the next logical step is to consider ways of addressing each. While some topics may be addressed through informal discussions and the sharing of ideas, others may require more expertise. In some cases, professional reading may provide answers and group members may volunteer to prepare for the meeting by reading selections relating to the topic.

In cases like this, it's usually a good idea to designate a discussion leader to keep the focus on the topic and to raise questions about the reading. The discussion leader often rotates from meeting to meeting, with each member eventually serving in this capacity. This means that longstanding members are not overburdened with responsibilities and new members are assimilated quickly and invited to contribute. Discussion leaders can also be used during informal meetings to keep the members on task and maintain the momentum.

Some topics may be addressed by speakers — classroom teachers from neighboring districts or schools, administrators, supervisors or college faculty — who possess expertise in a given area. When a speaker is invited, the topic and the group's level of expertise should be specified. If a classroom teacher, for example, is asked to talk about evaluation or assessment, he needs to know if the group is familiar with informal assessment techniques, such as running records or checklists, or if the members are just beginning to be concerned with alternative forms of evaluation. This will help him tailor his presentation to the group, avoiding miscommunication and frustration. It's also helpful for the group to prepare a questions, listed in order of priority, that they would like the speaker to address. This enables the speaker to prepare for the discussion and meet the group's expectations.

One teacher support group in New York State invited a speaker to discuss anecdotal records as an element of portfolio assessment. Knowing that their time was limited to 90 minutes, they asked the speaker to address the following questions:

- What information do you record?
- How often do you record information about each child? How much do you write?
- What formats do you suggest for maintaining records?
- How often do you review the records?

— How can they be used for parent conferences?
— What do you do with the records when the academic year is over?

As the speaker reviewed this list, she became aware of the group's concerns and planned her talk accordingly. She also noted that the group was concerned with the logistics of anecdotal records and planned to demonstrate how she incorporates the daily recording of her observations. She decided that her presentation would include many samples of records collected over time as well as her rationale for using the system she had developed.

AUDIOVISUAL AIDS

Whole language teachers find their colleagues are invaluable sources of information about new professional books, children's trade books and innovative strategies for implementing literature study. Often teachers find that audiovisual presentations bring ideas into sharper focus and answer questions more clearly than discussion or reading. While it may be difficult to view each other's classrooms in action, a vicarious visit is possible through presentations that include slides and tapes of children's activities as well as samples of their work, bulletin boards and learning centers.

Teachers can share their procedures for making things work and the rationale behind their classroom management techniques. Teachers who have managed to use limited space effectively and avoid clutter are a resource appreciated by their peers.

Audiotapes of literature study groups may be used to show how children responded to a new strategy. The tape enables others who are curious about how the groups function to hear for themselves and perhaps receive the encouragement and clarification they need to try literature study in their own classrooms. Because the teacher who made the tape is present, he can answer questions about the individuals involved and the activities that took place before and after the session.

Videotapes of classroom activities are popular because they allow teachers to see and hear strategies implemented under authentic classroom conditions. Techniques for conferring with writers and readers, for example, can be demonstrated very well on videotape because samples of the children's texts, their responses and the teacher's comments and questions can be seen simultaneously. Videotapes can be replayed as needed to answer questions and to inform new members about topics previously discussed. Some groups even maintain videotape libraries for their members.

Like discussions and sessions led by speakers, audiovisual presentations should be followed by a question-and-answer session. These enable group members to address specific questions, clarify information, expand on ideas and seek examples that apply to their own teaching situations. If sufficient time is allotted, individuals will leave the meeting feeling satisfied that their concerns have been addressed.

SHARING

The most important component of teacher-initiated support groups is sharing. This is recognized when time is set aside during meetings for teachers to share their best ideas, workable solutions and successes as well as their concerns. Every group member should receive a message that says, "Your way is okay!" Innovations on texts, ideas for creative response activities and techniques for exploring literature can be highlighted. Thematic units, complete with bibliographies, are resources worth sharing with others who should feel free to experiment with and add to them. Expanded units are often featured at future meetings where teachers are invited to explain how they adapted and integrated additional activities.

Teachers are always interested in the way others schedule classroom time. At a designated meeting, group members might be invited to bring copies of their daily or weekly schedules to discuss. If the group is large enough, smaller groups, designated by grade level, may meet to review schedules or design a workable composite from the samples. These small group sessions should be followed by a large group discussion where schedules can be reviewed.

Some time may also be set aside for a teacher to present a case study of a child who is experiencing difficulty. Group members often have valuable suggestions to offer as well as further questions to consider. The teacher making the presentation gains valuable insights and the group members benefit as their own perspectives are broadened.

Recently, Joyce, a teacher of 10-year-olds, brought a folder of Tony's writing samples to share with the group. She felt that Tony was stalled as a writer and wasn't sure how to help him. As she shared his drafts, copied on overhead transparencies, with the group, she talked briefly about each. To Joyce, it appeared that Tony did not revise his previous drafts, but started a brand new draft on the same topic at each writing session. She was clearly frustrated and asked for suggestions. Two members offered to role-play a conference with Tony to show Joyce how she could help him make revisions. Several suggestions were offered and, from these, Joyce decided to try asking Tony to cut apart his draft at the paragraph boundaries and experiment with alternative arrangements. She promised to share the outcome of her experiment at the next meeting.

During a coffee or tea break, informal sharing also takes place as members socialize. Mingling with fellow teachers can be enlightening and provide much-needed encouragement for the beginning whole language teacher. Time should be set aside during each meeting for socializing and becoming acquainted with new members who should always be helped to feel welcome and included. It is during these times that the informal networks so essential to the group's survival are formed.

How to Decide on a Group

If you are fortunate and live in an area where there are several support groups, you may attend a number of different meetings before you decide which one, if any, to join. It's important to find the best possible match between the group and your own needs. Begin by examining the members of each group. A group with members who teach various grade levels and possess a range of experience with whole language may be more valuable to you than one where the membership is homogeneous. On the other hand, a group composed of teachers at roughly the same stage of implementing whole language may be able to address more of your concerns than one that is more diverse. Obviously, it's also helpful to know whether the group is accepting new members.

A second important consideration is the goals of the group. These may be defined in a document such as a constitution or, informally, in a pamphlet. For example, if the group advocates addressing political concerns such as lobbying local, regional or national officials, is this a goal you're comfortable supporting? The group's orientation may be towards providing inservice opportunities that are not available through official channels. A clue to the group's responsiveness to its membership may be indicated by the topics on the program — are they static or do they change from year to year?

As a beginning whole language teacher, you may not have access to many materials or resources for starting your program. If this is the case, an important consideration when choosing a group is the resources it offers its members. Ask about the number and copyright dates of resources in the group's professional lending library. Are there just a few outdated books or is there an extensive supply of current titles? Both the topics and the resources may speak volumes about the group. Does the group maintain a supply of big books, multiple copies of children's trade books or other resources, such as read-along tapes for members to check out for use in their own classrooms? The ability to test resources before you buy or order them is a definite advantage of group membership.

While affiliation with a larger group or organization doesn't guarantee that a group is worthwhile, it often provides a vehicle for tapping into information about programs, speakers and materials. Affiliation with the Whole Language Umbrella or the IRA Whole Language Special Interest Group may introduce you to resources beyond your immediate geographical area through penpals, newsletters and meetings of affiliated groups. Some teacher-support groups have grown so large that they've organized satellite groups to help teachers feel more comfortable. The satellite groups then come together for regularly scheduled meetings at which major speakers can be featured. Expenses are divided among the satellite groups.

Only you can decide whether a particular group is for you. Once you've attended meetings of several groups, think about how well you fit in with the other members, how comfortable you are with the format of the meetings and how well-matched the group is to your current needs and interests. If none feels exactly right, remember you can always start your own group!

Enjoy Your Journey

During your first year of exploring whole language, you'll experience many changes, some of them uplifting, others discouraging. Maintaining what feels like forward motion may be difficult if you try to go it alone. If there is no one in your school who can share your joys as well as your frustrations, you may be tempted to give up before you really get started. Like all learners, you need a consistent source of feedback to know how you're doing.

One way to help you keep your perspective and grow professionally is to share your concerns and ideas with other interested individuals. The members of your support group are essential companions on your journey towards whole language. Not only can they help you survive, they can also help you thrive as you chart your way through new territory. While not every teacher follows exactly the same path towards whole language, everyone finds their own journey interesting, exciting, rewarding — and worth sharing.

APPENDIX 1

Checklist for a Whole Language Classroom Environment

What are the quiet areas and how are they designated?

_____ Book Corner
_____ Computer and Printer Workstation
_____ Writing Center
_____ Listening Station with headphones
_____ Other

How do children use the book corner?

_____ Browse through books
_____ Relax and read independently
_____ Share books with friends
_____ Look for comment cards/recommendations from peers
_____ Check out books to read elsewhere
_____ Read books by classroom authors

How is the computer station used?

_____ Drafting children's texts (individual)
_____ Revising children's drafts (individual)
_____ Collaborative writing by pairs of children
_____ Revising collaborative drafts
_____ Editing drafts (individual)
_____ Editing drafts (collaborative)
_____ Illustrating drafts (individual)
_____ Illustrating drafts (collaborative)
_____ Publishing drafts (individual)
_____ Publishing drafts (collaborative)
_____ Playing games
_____ Other

What activities take place at the writing center?

____ Experimenting with spelling using magnetic letters
____ Creating texts with stamp pads and letters
____ Making or binding books
____ Writing letters to friends and family
____ Creating signs or labels
____ Copying texts from books
____ Illustrating texts
____ Drafting texts for wordless books

____ Adding to a class cumulative story/chart
____ Tracing letters/stencils

How is the listening station/post used?

____ Group read-along with individual tape of big books
____ Group read-along with tapes of trade books
____ Individual read-alongs with self-selected tapes
____ Acting out story with puppets and props

What activities take place in other quiet areas?

____ Sharing flannelboard stories
____ Reading or creating movie rolls of stories
____ Reading charts/experience stories

Where are the active areas and how are they designated (signs/rules/furniture/materials)?

_____ Math Manipulatives Center
_____ Block/ Construction Corner
_____ Science Exploration Area
_____ Arts/Crafts Workspace
_____ Puppet Theatre
_____ Game or Play Area

How do children work in each area?

Math Manipulatives Center
_____ Problem-solving (individual)
_____ Problem-solving (peers)
_____ Designing problems for others
_____ Researching problems in books
_____ Recording solutions

Block/Construction Corner
_____ Creating models based on topics in books
_____ Exploring space and materials
_____ Collaborative building with peers
_____ Labeling products
_____ Planning long-term projects
_____ Consulting book sources for verification

Science Exploration Area
_____ Manipulating materials
_____ Observing outcomes
_____ Recording observations/experiments
_____ Consulting sources for experiments

_____ Collaborating on experiments
_____ Compiling group data
_____ Designing experiments

Arts and Crafts Workspace
_____ Illustrating an original text
_____ Illustrating a collaborative text
_____ Making a mural
_____ Creating puppets
_____ Making models
_____ Exploring media
_____ Creating collages
_____ Weaving
_____ Origami
_____ Assembling jackdaws
_____ Making paper

Puppet Theater
_____ Performing plots of familiar stories
_____ Performing plots of original stories
_____ Inventing alternative plots to folktales
_____ Planning and drafting puppet plays
_____ Rehearsing original plays
_____ Improvising with variety of puppets
_____ Consulting books for story ideas

Game or Play Area
_____ Playing individual games
_____ Creating a variation of familiar game
_____ Role-playing a social situation or problem
_____ Role-playing careers (clerk, waiter, police officer, etc.)
_____ Making game boards or pieces
_____ Consulting rule books for alternatives
_____ Creating a game based on book or author

Notes

APPENDIX 2

Sample Record Page Using Self-Sticking Notes

NAME Marla S.

ADDRESS 29 Evans St. TELEPHONE

BIRTHDATE 8/7/ AGE 6 GRADE 1

Marla is an only child. She is read to a lot at home. She uses clues for comprehension and is writing her full name. Uses inventive spelling and first/last letters.

9/21 Read big book and noticed that all sentences started with "I"

10/20 Recognized wd "truck" in predictable story and again in our "new" story

11/20 M's written story was well-sequenced - had beginning, middle + end.

10/5 Predicted masked wds. in sentences

11/7 Can recognize many common sight wds. e.g., you, the, here, am.

APPENDIX 3

Portfolio Assessment Record Writing Sample

clinic
Molly and I come to reading clinck every Tuesday.

bank
I am doing my word beak.

I am reading a book.

started carve pumpkin
I've storted to korv a Ponkin

This pumpkin done
Thes is when the Popkin is all don

made spiders Halloween
We maed Spoeds for Hollowen

This
Thes is When we are working on the
computer
conpotr.

cards
I am doing my Word Cords.

I'm reading The WHINGDINGDILLY.

clinic
The reading clinck is fun.

Paul knows to:

Capitalize the first word in a sentence
use periods at the end of sentences.
Capitalize Halloween

All the sentences are complete sentences!

Paul learned to:

underline the title of a book.

APPENDIX 4

Sample Diagnostic Reading Checklist

NAME________________________________ DATE______________________

GRADE_______ AGE________ OBSERVER_________________________________

1 — Never 2 — Sometimes 3 — Frequently 4 — Not Observed

ENJOYMENT OF BOOKS

Enjoys books alone	_____
Enjoys books with an adult	_____
Interested in books	_____
Listens to stories	_____
Enjoys a range of reading — fiction, non-fiction, magazines, etc.	_____

READING BEHAVIOR

Chooses to read alone in free time	_____
Reads willingly to others	_____
Feels confident as a reader	_____
Expects books to be meaningful	_____
Expects books to be fun	_____
"Reads" familiar text from memory	_____
Reads unfamiliar text	_____
Reads orally with fluency	_____
Reads silently	_____

PRINT CONVENTIONS

Knows literary conventions — title, author, illustrator, chapter, etc.	_____
Observes and understands end punctuation — period, question mark, exclamation mark	_____
Observes and understands internal punctuation — comma, semi-colon, colon, ellipsis	_____
Observes and understands quotation marks	_____

Developed by Stephen Phelps and Carol Hodges, Buffalo State College, New York

APPENDIX 5

Sample Checklist for Writing

NAME________________________________ DATE_____________________

GRADE_______ AGE_______ OBSERVER______________________________

Key
Yes (most of the time)
No (not an observable behavior)

	YES	NO
TOPIC SELECTION		
Thinks of ideas to write about	_____	_____
Participates in brainstorming activities	_____	_____
Show interest in writing about chosen topics	_____	_____
Thinks of words/terms related to topic	_____	_____
Organizes ideas before drafting	_____	_____
· constructs word webs (maps)	_____	_____
· constructs an outline	_____	_____
· list words/terms and groups	_____	_____
Has imaginative ideas	_____	_____
DRAFTING		
Writes complete sentences	_____	_____
Writes similar ideas in a paragraph	_____	_____
Uses or attempts punctuation	_____	_____
· period	_____	_____
· question mark	_____	_____
· quotation marks	_____	_____
· capital letters	_____	_____
Skips lines for purpose of revising	_____	_____
Writes about chosen topic, doesn't stray	_____	_____
Writes topic sentence	_____	_____
Ideas are related, not merely enumerated	_____	_____

REVISING

Revises sequence of ideas if necessary _____ _____
Expands ideas to clarify meaning _____ _____
· uses modifiers _____ _____
· compound sentences _____ _____
· complex sentences _____ _____
Shortens sentences to clarify and simplify _____ _____
Shares and discusses writing _____ _____
· with an adult (teacher) _____ _____
· with another child (peer) _____ _____
· with a group of children (peers) _____ _____
Examines written product and asks questions _____ _____
· Are all the sentences about the topic? _____ _____
· Is the intended meaning conveyed? _____ _____
· Did I write for an audience? _____ _____

EDITING

Checks for —
correct punctuation _____ _____
complete sentences _____ _____
appropriate sequence _____ _____
capitalization _____ _____
· first word of sentence _____ _____
· proper nouns _____ _____
· pronoun, I _____ _____
period at end of sentence _____ _____
first word of paragraph indented _____ _____
spelling conventions _____ _____

PUBLISHING

Shows interest in publishing _____ _____
Participates in making a publishable product _____ _____
Enjoys sharing written stories with others _____ _____

APPENDIX 6

Sample Checklist for Emergent Writing

NAME__________________________________ DATE_______________________

GRADE_______ AGE________ OBSERVER__________________________________

Key
Yes (most of the time)
No (not an observable behavior)

	YES	NO
The child —		
draws pictures	_____	_____
scribbles to communicate	_____	_____
reads own scribble writing	_____	_____
writes some letters	_____	_____
uses same letters in different sequence to represent different words	_____	_____
writes first letter of words	_____	_____
writes first and last letters of words	_____	_____
writes first, last and middle letters	_____	_____
writes vowel letters	_____	_____
spells some common sight words from memory	_____	_____
spells most words phonetically	_____	_____
uses print conventions	_____	_____
· capitalization (I and first letter of sentence)	_____	_____
· period	_____	_____
Length of story —		
· word and picture	_____	_____
· phrase and picture	_____	_____
· one sentence	_____	_____
· two-three sentences	_____	_____
· four-five sentences	_____	_____

APPENDIX 7

Sample Checklists for Speaking and Listening

NAME________________________________ DATE______________________

GRADE_______ AGE________ OBSERVER________________________________

Key
Yes (most of the time)
No (not an observable behavior)

	YES	NO
SPEAKING		
The child can —		
convey a message to a listener	_____	_____
describe objects or events	_____	_____
place events of a story or message in sequence	_____	_____
formulate questions	_____	_____
retell a story by including the beginning, middle and end	_____	_____
use language to socialize with other children	_____	_____
use a variety of sentence patterns	_____	_____
include emotion in speech	_____	_____
LISTENING		
The child —		
shows enjoyment when listening to stories	_____	_____
listens to and follows oral directions with minimal assistance	_____	_____
listens to peers and responds to their comments during conversations	_____	_____
listens to a variety of oral presentations (e.g., tapes, records, peers)	_____	_____
discriminates among environmental sounds (e.g., music, speech, animal noises, phonemes)	_____	_____

APPENDIX 8

Sample Reading and Writing Logs

READING LOG

NAME Mark Z. AGE 9 GRADE 3

Date 11/2

Book	Author	Pages	Comments	Rec.
James and the Giant Peach	R. Dahl	200	A great book about Ja and his travels	+

ALARM CLOCK READING LOG

NAME Pamjit S. AGE 9 GRADE 3

Book Charlotte's Web Author E.B. White

Week of March 10

	Mon.	Tues.	Wed.	Thurs.	Fri.
Pages Read	1-19	20-28	29-40	41-53	54-65

Comments A great book. I'm worried about Wilbur. I wonder if Charlotte can really save him.

WRITING LOG

NAME Sam P. AGE 8 GRADE 2

Date 9/20 No ideas
9/22 Airplanes
9/24 Fall leaves
9/26 Apples
9/27 wrote words about apples
10/27 Two sentences on apples

APPENDIX 9

Sample Reading Interview

What is reading?

What do you do when you come to a word you don't recognize?

What do you do when you read something that doesn't make sense?

How do you learn new words?

Do you think you're a good reader? Why?

Who is the best reader in the class? How do you know?

Why is learning to read important?

What is your favorite story or book?

How do you feel when you're asked to read out loud?

Do you prefer reading out loud or to yourself?

How do you choose books for independent reading?

How do you feel about your reading group?

What do you do during reading time in your classroom?

How do you go about completing worksheets or dittos?

Do worksheets help you understand stories?

Do worksheets help you learn new words?

Do you enjoy listening to stories?

APPENDIX 10

Sample Writing Interview

What is writing?

Write something now (*hand child blank sheet of paper*). Where do you start writing? What did you write?

Do you write at home? What do you write about?

Do you write at school? What do you write about?

What does a good writer do?

Who is a good writer in the class? How do you know?

When you come to a word that you don't know how to write, what do you do?

Do you like to write? Why?

What do you like to write about?

Do you keep a journal or diary?

Do you have a place where you can read or write?

Why do we use (*show punctuation*) in writing?

What is this (*show a paragraph and outline it with your finger*) called? Why are all the sentences together?

Which is harder for you — reading or writing? Why?

If you were going to teach or help someone to write, what would you do?

What's the hardest thing about writing? The easiest?

Does writing help you read? How?

Do you ever change what you're writing? How do you decide what to change?

How do you know when a piece of writing is finished?

Have you ever received a letter? What kind?

BIBLIOGRAPHY

Understanding Whole Language

Froese, V. (Ed.) *Whole Language Practice and Theory.* Scarborough, Ontario: Prentice-Hall Canada, 1990.

This introductory text is a useful tool for novice whole language teachers who want to learn how to structure, plan and execute a whole language program. It provides an operational definition of whole language but its aim clearly is to present readers with meaningful classroom learning activities. Topics covered include talk, literature, writing and drama, ideas for organizing a whole language environment and wholistic assessment. The final chapter reviews and presents research about whole language in an easily understandable manner.

Goodman, K. *What's Whole in Whole Language: A Parent/Teacher's Guide to Children's Learning.* Portsmouth, New Hampshire: Heinemann, 1986.

In this readable whole language primer, Goodman shares current theories about language acquisition as he helps readers understand why this philosophy is in line with recent developments in the cognitive sciences. Goodman also addresses practical issues. He describes his views of a whole language classroom, a whole language teacher and a whole language curriculum. Throughout the text, he stresses that whole language is a set of beliefs regarding the way children learn that can be translated into instructional practices in various ways. An excellent first selection for those interested in understanding the whole language movement.

Watson, D., Burke, C., & Harste, J. *Whole Language: Inquiring Voices.* Richmond Hill, Ontario: Scholastic-TAB, 1989.

In the preface to this book, the authors state that it was written in an attempt to help classroom teachers "understand inquiry as a way of understanding children in classrooms, and the teaching-learning relationship as one in which children act as informants." They describe the conditions necessary for inquiry and provide suggestions for beginning teacher-researchers. The book concludes with a series of stories that are "invitations and encouragements" to emergent whole language researchers.

Weaver, C. *Understanding Whole Language: From Principles to Practice*. Portsmouth, New Hampshire: Heinemann, 1990.

Weaver aims to provide educators with an understanding of whole language, including its theoretical underpinnings, research base and instructional implications. She has taken great care to provide thorough explanations in an attempt to combat misconceptions regarding the whole language movement. Weaver defines whole language, describes how the development of whole language teachers can be fostered, and explains how to create whole language classrooms.

Whole Language Journeys: Personal Accounts

Atwell, N. *In the Middle: Writing, Reading and Learning with Adolescents*. Portsmouth, New Hampshire: Heinemann, 1987.

Nancy Atwell uses her gifts as a writer to tell how she made the transition from an "assignment-giver" to a teacher who interacted with and learned from her students. A step-by-step approach is not for Atwell, who has learned to teach through immersion. Readers are provided with details of mini-lessons, reading-writing conferences, scheduling and grading as they evolved in her classroom. Although Atwell was working with adolescents, her book has significant implications for all K-12 teachers.

Bird, L. (Ed.) *Becoming a Whole Language School: The Fair Oaks Story*. Katonah, New York: Richard C. Owen, 1989.

This is a first-hand account of Fair Oaks Elementary School's journey towards whole language. Readers are provided with various points of view as they listen to the voices of teachers, the principal, the superintendent, research consultants and a school board member, all of whom worked together to make the transition possible. Teachers discuss such topics as escaping from their basals, putting phonics in its proper place, teaching reading and writing and finding their own way through the transition process.

Mills, H. & Clyde, J.A. (Eds.) *Portraits of Whole Language Classrooms: Learning for All Ages*. Portsmouth, New Hampshire: Heinemann, 1990.

A diverse group of whole language teachers working with students from preschool to college levels and populations of varying abilities describe a day in their whole language classrooms. Strategies for implementing whole language are revealed through description, classroom vignettes, samples of students' work and the teachers' reflections. This excellent text is highly recommended for the novice concerned about the organization of whole language classrooms.

Newman, J. (Ed.) *Whole Language: Theory in Use*. Portsmouth, New Hampshire: Heinemann, 1985.

This anthology was compiled to help whole language teachers with "how-to" questions dealing with the implications of whole language theory in classrooms. The articles are written by teachers who have themselves tried to understand current research and communicate what's involved in "creating and sustaining a whole language environment." Topics include the research implications for a whole language curriculum, using children's books to teach reading, journal writing, letter writing, spelling, holding conferences, text organization and activity cards.

Newman, J.M. (Ed.) *Finding Our Own Way: Teachers Exploring Their Assumptions*. Portsmouth, New Hampshire: Heinemann, 1990.

This collection of 23 articles highlights the struggles and aspirations of classroom teachers dealing with the practical implications of their whole language philosophies. Readers will identify with the different paths the authors have taken toward child-centered curriculums and come to understand that the journey towards whole language is very personal. The articles provide support and encouragement to those attempting to implement whole language in their classrooms.

Routman, R. *Transitions: From Literature to Literacy*. Portsmouth, New Hampshire: Heinemann, 1988.

Transitions is a must for all educators who want to incorporate whole language methods in their classrooms, but aren't sure where to begin. Routman bridges the gap between theory and practice as she recounts her own professional journey towards a wholistic language arts curriculum. She shares daily schedules, wholistic strategies, synopses of her favorite children's books, alternatives to seatwork, creative extension activities and evaluation methods. The appendixes, which include numerous professional resources, are invaluable.

Sourcebooks

Baskwill, J. & Whitman, P. *Whole Language Sourcebook: A Guide for Teachers of Grades One and Two.* Richmond Hill, Ontario: Scholastic-TAB, 1986.

This definitive guide is an excellent source of information for first- and second-grade teachers interested in implementing whole language activities in their classrooms. The first of three sections deals with daily routines for shared language time, the teacher-directed section of Baskwill and Whitman's whole language program. Clear directions, diagrams and photographs enhance the descriptions of activities presented. Perhaps the most ambitious section of this guide is the second, which focuses on themed units. Several of these are provided, complete with daily lesson plans and literary resources. This kind of detail is perfect for teachers who are apprehensive about teaching themes for the first time. The authors conclude with a section offering valuable insights into classroom management.

Baskwill, J. & Whitman, P. *Moving On: Whole Language Sourcebook for Grades Three and Four.* Richmond Hill, Ontario: Scholastic-TAB, 1988.

Baskwill and Whitman's second sourcebook is written for educators wrestling with the implementation of whole language beyond the primary grades. The guide's introductory section on classroom management suggests "comfortable" ways to break into whole language teaching. Ideas for organizing class time will provide structure to help teachers until they feel confident about developing schedules of their own. A second section on routines suggests wholistic language arts strategies and activities appropriate for the junior grades. Readers looking for concrete examples of units will be delighted with the manual's third section, which presents four themes complete with detailed descriptions of daily lessons. A chapter on evaluation concludes the book.

Watson, D. (Ed.) *Ideas and Insights: Language Arts in the Elementary School.* Urbana, Illinois: National Council of Teachers of English, 1987.

Dorothy Watson says, "Language is learned as children use it in reading, writing, listening, and speaking about science, math, and social studies, and as they transact with their world and the people in it." This is the philosophy behind this ambitious resource that contains more than 200 curriculum-spanning language activities for students in elementary and secondary school. Along with specific directions, activity descriptions include a rationale and suggested grade level appropriateness. A chapter dealing with evaluation will help teachers assess children's development as language users. A bibliography of recommended books, including read-alouds, wordless books and predictable books, is also included.

The Reading-Writing Connection

Atwell, N. (Ed.) *Coming to Know: Writing to Learn in the Intermediate Grades*. Portsmouth, New Hampshire: Heinemann, 1990.

The contributors — teachers of grades three through six— share strategies for adding a personal dimension to content area writing. These strategies offer alternatives to traditional content area report assignments and illustrate beautifully how the writing process can be applied across the curriculum. An excellent series of appendixes sets out genres for report writing, prompts for learning log entries, children's literature for content area study and resources for writing and reading to learn.

Moore, D., Moore, S.A., Cunningham, P. & Cunningham, J.W. *Developing Readers and Writers in the Content Areas: K-12*. White Plains, New York: Longman, 1986.

Ideas for integrating reading and writing with content area subjects are presented to teachers from primary grades through secondary school. In chapter one, the authors discuss the thinking processes that contribute to learning. The balance of the book demonstrates how these processes underlie the teaching strategies and methods presented. The first seven chapters explain methods of instruction while the remainder is the fictional account of how four teachers spent a school year developing readers and writers in the content areas. Although the situations are contrived, they provide useful illustrations of the examples mentioned.

Stewig, J.W. *Read to Write: Using Children's Literature as a Springboard for Teaching Writing*. 3rd Edition. Katonah, New York: Richard C. Owen, 1990.

Stewig presents a writing program that focuses on developing children's skill in writing different kinds of fiction and poetry by building their understanding and appreciation of literature. His three-part strategy begins by presenting students with a rich variety of literature, then guides them to interact with the literature and finally invites them to create their own stories and poems based on their guided literary experiences. The book includes children's writing samples as well as synopses of quality children's books.

Teaching Writing

Graves, D. *Writing: Teachers and Children at Work*. Portsmouth, New Hampshire: Heinemann, 1983.

Don't make the mistake of overlooking this resource because of its copyright date. The book is actually a collection of workshops that Graves has compiled in book form to assist classroom teachers with teaching children's writing. Based on a three-year study of children's writing funded by the National Institute of Education, Graves shares his wealth of experience as he discusses the teacher's role in the writing process, children's growth as they are engaged in the writing process, and issues dealing with recording and reporting student's writing progress. A classic text for teachers interested in obtaining insight into the writing process.

Villiers, U. *Luk Mume Luk Dade I Kan Rit*. Richmond Hill, Ontario: Scholastic-TAB, 1989.

Villiers has compiled an exciting and delightful anthology of primary children's writing collected over a three-year period. The book includes reproductions of the original works, some of them in color, categorized according to the developmental stages of the child authors. As Villiers shares her insights into each piece, readers begin to recognize the developmental stages of children's writing and become attuned to the process of naturalistic writing evaluation.

Walshe, R.D. *Every Child Can Write!* Rosebery, Australia: Primary English Teaching Association, 1988.

Walshe believes that all children can write and that they learn to write by writing. In straightforward terms, he describes what he calls "the essential simplicities of teaching/learning writing." Chapter topics include descriptions of the writing process, the writing environment, the conference approach to writing and ideas for maximizing children's sense of ownership over topics. Graphics complement the text throughout. An excellent resource for novice whole language teachers.

Emergent Literacy

Beginning Reading. Victoria, Australia: Ministry of Education, 1986.

This 40-page guide to teaching reading was written by teachers, for teachers. Produced by the Infant Education Committee of the Primary Schools Division in Victoria, the booklet describes reading as a natural developmental process in which skills are acquired as children express their own direct experiences. The authors suggest that beginning reading materials should contain language patterns and events children are familiar with. They explain the cuing systems involved in reading and present ideas for talking and listening, building enthusiasm for reading, getting to know the language of literature, developing awareness of print and organizing for reading and evaluation.

Holdaway, D. *Foundations of Literacy*. New York: Scholastic, 1979.

Holdaway begins this classic book by describing a developmental model of literacy. His discussion of literacy development before school includes illustrative dialogues by children at various stages of reading development. He discusses the implications of his model for formal schooling and includes an explanation of the shared reading experience, the cuing systems involved in the reading process and strategies for teaching reading at various developmental stages.

Morrow, L. *Literacy Development in the Early Years: Helping Children Read and Write*. Englewood Cliffs, New Jersey: Prentice-Hall, 1989.

This articulate text shares a perceptive view of early literacy that represents "cutting-edge" research. Initial chapters provide the theoretical framework that has influenced recent programs for the emergent literate and address the influence of the home on young language learners. Remaining chapters deal with specific areas of literacy development, including oral language, reading and writing as well as ideas for organizing a conducive classroom environment. Each chapter includes an overview of relevant research, suggested teaching strategies, assessment procedures and activity suggestions. Detailed appendixes list materials and resources that will be invaluable for both parents and teachers.

Strickland, D.S. & Morrow, L.M. (Eds.) *Emerging Literacy: Young Children Learn to Read and Write*. Newark, Delaware: International Reading Association, 1989.

Contemporary researchers, renowned for their work in children's literacy development, contributed to this volume on emergent literacy. The book presents theoretical and research perspectives as well as practical suggestions appropriate for children aged two to eight. Topics include the shared reading experience, the implications of a whole language paradigm, the use of children's literature, the school literacy environment and the nature of wholistic assessment. A photo essay written by classroom teachers implementing whole language techniques in their classrooms is exceptionally interesting.

Learning to Use Literature in the Classroom

Cullinan, B. (Ed.) *Children's Literature in the Reading Program*. Newark, Delaware: International Reading Association,1987.

Contributors to this collection of articles are familiar names in the field of children's literature and reading. The book provides suggestions for introducing and sustaining a literature program as well as for books that can be used as "starters." Readings provide a rationale for using children's literature in the reading program and describe reading programs that use literature in the primary, junior and intermediate grades.

Johnson, T.D. & Louis, D.R. *Literacy through Literature.* Portsmouth, New Hampshire: Heinemann, 1987.

This text describes a wealth of practical strategies for incorporating the best in children's literature into classroom programs. Activities are presented for the emergent literate as well as the developing reader. A handy text in an appealing format.

Lamme, L. (Ed.) *Learning to Love Literature: Preschool through Grade 3.* Urbana, Illinois: National Council of Teachers of English, 1981.

This well-organized, comprehensive text was originally developed to help early childhood teachers make children's literature the core of their curriculums. Topics covered include creating a literature-rich environment, employing wholistic teaching strategies, storytelling and integrating literature across the curriculum. In one chapter, eight early childhood and primary teachers share their experiences with using literature as an integral part of their curriculum, helping the reader understand the classroom applications of the procedures suggested. An excellent chapter on print and nonprint resources for a literature program is also provided.

Short, K. & Pierce, K. (Eds.) *Talking about Books: Creating Literate Communities.* Portsmouth, New Hampshire: Heinemann, 1990.

This anthology of articles was written by educators who share a common belief "in the power of dialogue within a community of learners." Collaborative strategies for encouraging talk about books and creating a literate community that uses books to learn are presented.

Stewig, J.W. & Sebesta, S. *Using Literature in the Elementary Classroom.* 2nd Edition. Urbana, Illinois: National Council of Teachers of English, 1989.

When the first edition of this text appeared a decade ago, Stewig and Sebesta were ahead of their time in proposing not only the integration of reading with the other language arts, but also the integration of language across the curriculum. This second edition has been compiled to help teachers implement a wholistic curriculum where literature is placed at the center of instruction. The articulate text presents numerous creative and practical ideas and suggests many titles for classroom use as well as related or additional teacher resources.

Themed Units

Pappas, C., Kiefer, B. & Levstik, L. *An Integrated Language Perspective in the Elementary School.* White Plains, New York: Longman, 1990.

An integrated language perspective on teaching in the elementary school is outlined in this text that provides comprehensive coverage of thematic units. Chapters address issues such as planning and implementing thematic units in the classroom, "kid-watching" procedures, evaluating student performance and planning for school-wide change based on integrated language procedures. Eight prototypes for thematic units appropriate for various levels from K-8 are illustrated and explained. Excellent professional and children's resources are suggested for each unit.

Moss, J.F. *Focus Units in Literature: A Handbook for Elementary School Teachers.* Urbana, Illinois: National Council of Teachers of English, 1984.

Moss has designed an instructional model that provides a framework for creating a context for literacy. Her model is translated into classroom practice through literature, or focus, units designed to be used from kindergarten through grade six. Each unit centers around a theme that uses literature to develop language and thinking skills. An excellent resource for teachers who want explicit guidelines for planning themed units.

Moss, J.F. *Focus on Literature: A Context for Literacy Learning.* Katonah, New York: Richard C. Owen, 1990.

Moss presents a series of literature, or focus, units in this text that provides a framework for encouraging "literacy, language and thinking skills" within the social context of the classroom. While the first two chapters present the theoretical framework for focus units and discuss the importance of classroom dialogue, most of the text is devoted to the units themselves. Each unit, which is structured around a central theme, introduces literary genres that parallel students' interests at various grade levels. The units are complementary, each highlighting the development of whole language techniques and strategies such as the child-centered classroom, literacy across the curriculum, the reading-writing relationship and so on.

Reading Strategies

Holdaway, D. *Independence in Reading*. 2nd Edition. New York: Scholastic, 1980.

Although this text was designed to be a handbook of practical teaching suggestions, the ideas are presented in the context of a sound theoretical framework. Holdaway discusses classroom organization and teaching strategies that encourage reading independence and incorporates a wide range of children's literature into his suggested activities.

Lynch, P. *Using Big Books and Predictable Books*. Richmond Hill, Ontario: Scholastic-TAB, 1986.

This concise primer is perfect for teachers who are just beginning to introduce big books and predictable books into their reading programs. Short- and long-term planning suggestions are provided and the seven-day sequence of activities can easily be adapted to individual teacher preferences.

Peetoom, Adrian. *Shared Reading: Safe Risks with Whole Books*. Richmond Hill, Ontario: Scholastic-TAB, 1986.

Peetoom's guide is designed to help less confident readers in grades two through six make the transition from reading short stories to reading chapter books. His "safety-netting" techniques have been carefully selected to lend support and encouragement to students who have a tendency to doubt themselves. Teachers will find the strategies presented useful for helping all children become independent readers.

Wilson, L. *Write Me a Sign about Language Experience*. Melbourne, Australia: Nelson Australia, 1979.

Lorraine Wilson has written a practical text that explains how language experience can be used to enhance literacy development. Written from the perspective of her own experience as vice-principal of an inner-suburban school, the book succinctly sets out a rationale and explanation for the language experience approach. Wilson explains how to motivate children so they see a purpose in reading and writing and provides ideas for stimulating language development in the classroom.

The book also provides an outline for a suggested literacy course. This handy text thoroughly explains an approach that is often overlooked or abused.

Spelling Instruction

Gentry, J.R. *Spel Is a Four-Letter Word*. Richmond Hill, Ontario: Scholastic-TAB, 1987.

Gentry dispels the myths surrounding spelling instruction by pointing out that they have no research-based reality. He describes the developmental stages of spelling and provides guidelines for recognizing when a child is ready for formal spelling instruction. He also answers teachers' most commonly asked questions about spelling instruction — including how to help children learn to spell words that have been missed on spelling tests. A section containing advice for parents is extremely helpful.

Buchanan, E. *Spelling for Whole Language Classrooms*. Winnipeg, Manitoba: Whole Language Consultants, 1989. (Available from Richard C. Owen, Katonah, New York.)

Buchanan stresses that spelling is a developmental process and attempts to make connections between a theory of spelling development, instruction and evaluation. Her discussion of a whole language spelling curriculum includes guidelines for spelling instruction, a description of the stages of spelling development and instructional strategies for each developmental stage, and suggestions for initiating quantitative and qualitative analysis, including a procedure for "misspelling analysis."

Hudson, C. & O'Toole, M. *Spelling: A Teacher's Guide*. Victoria, Australia: Landmark Educational Supplies, 1990.

This text was designed to respond to teachers' questions about spelling instruction. The authors stress that spelling is a part of the total language arts program and demands a "flexible, informal and systematic teaching approach." The link between the process of developing children's writing and the teaching of spelling is also addressed. A theoretical base for spelling instruction and implications for teaching are provided. Practical ideas presented include suggestions for developing spelling lists, teaching spelling in context, employing creative strategies and activities, creating a spelling environment, involving parents in the spelling program and evaluating student progress.

Whole Language and Special Populations

Rhodes, L.K. & Dudley-Marley, C. *Readers and Writers with a Difference.* Portsmouth, New Hampshire: Heinemann, 1988.

The authors present strategies to encourage the reading and writing development of learning disabled and remedial readers as well as "an observational approach to reading and writing assessment." Special chapters are devoted to writing meaningful instructional goals and objectives, planning lessons from a wholistic perspective, collaborating with parents, classroom teachers and administrators, and structuring the learning environment. Bibliographies include lists of predictable books for primary and junior grade children.

Whole Language and the Arts

McCaslin, N. *Creative Drama in the Classroom.* White Plains, New York: Longman, 1990.

Creative Drama in the Classroom is a clear, precise handbook of activities ranging from beginning exercises for the imagination to suggestions for creating and producing plays. Poems, folktales and stories are provided that can be used for activities such as choral readings, reader's theatre and so on. McCaslin says she chose activities to "develop concentration, imagination, and use of voice, body and speech." Sections of special interest include discussions of drama as a teaching tool and creative drama for children with special needs. A readable text that emphasizes practice.

Evaluation

Baskwill, J. & Whitman, P. *Evaluation: Whole Language, Whole Child.* Richmond Hill, Ontario: Scholastic-TAB, 1988.

This 41-page guide goes a long way towards empowering teachers to become evaluators in their whole language classrooms. The authors describe useful and manageable alternatives to basal end-of-book and standardized tests. Wholistic procedures are described in straightforward terms and ideas for scheduling observational assessments and reporting to parents are also included.

Clay, M. *The Early Detection of Reading Difficulties*. Portsmouth, New Hampshire: Heinemann, 1985.

The first portion of this useful volume describes an evaluative tool for systematically observing young readers. Clay sets out how to make a running record and ideas for assessing letter identification, knowledge of concepts relating to print, word knowledge and writing behavior. Guidelines for summarizing diagnostic survey results are also described. The second part of the text describes the reading recovery program, an early intervention program for young children experiencing difficulty with beginning reading. The text concludes with six research reports, each of which address the effects of various aspects of the reading recovery program. An invaluable diagnostic tool for teachers interested in evaluating young readers wholistically.

Goodman, K., Goodman, Y. & Hood, W. (Eds.) *The Whole Language Evaluation Book*. Portsmouth, New Hampshire: Heinemann, 1989.

The editors have compiled articles rich in classroom vignettes, providing examples of incidental, informal and formal evaluation in a variety of whole language settings. Beginning chapters deal with the research and theoretical base for whole language evaluation. Because the editors perceive evaluation as an integral part of the curriculum, subsequent chapters do not separate evaluation from the teaching-learning process. And because evaluation techniques are embedded in daily classroom activities, the book also supplies readers with ideas for organizing a whole language program.

Goodman, Y., Watson, D. & Burke, C. *Reading Miscue Inventory: Alternative Procedures*. Katonah, New York: Richard C. Owen, 1987.

This assessment package describes miscue analysis, including its historical underpinnings and an overview of the model of reading upon which it is based. Four alternative procedures for miscue analysis are provided. The reader meets Betsy, whose oral reading serves as a prototype for miscue analysis throughout the book. The final portion of the text describes how miscue analysis provides insights that can be used to make decisions regarding curriculum development and instructional procedures.

Spandel, V. & Stiggins, R.J. *Creating Writers: Linking Assessment and Writing Instruction*. White Plains, New York: Longman, 1990.

The authors believe that the missing link in writing instruction has been everyday assessment techniques that, when used by teachers and students, connect to effective writing instruction. Therefore, they provide readers with a resource for writing evaluation that includes a clear set of standards for what constitutes good writing, examples of wholistic and analytical evaluative procedures, and strategies for writing instruction. Sample protocols provide readers with the opportunity to apply described scoring procedures, interpret results and compare their interpretations with those provided by the authors.

Additional Professional Resources

UNDERSTANDING WHOLE LANGUAGE

Altwerger, B. et. al. "Whole Language: What's New?" In *The Reading Teacher.*Vol. 41, no. 2 (1987).

Farris, P. & Kaczmarski, D. "Whole Language: A Closer Look." In *Contemporary Education*. Vol. 59, no. 2 (1988).

Fields, M. "Talking and Writing: Explaining the Whole Language Approach to Parents." In *The Reading Teacher*. Vol. 41, no.9 (1988).

Fountas, I. & Hannigan, I. "Making Sense of Whole Language: The Pursuit of Informed Teaching." In *Childhood Education*, Vol. 65, no. 3 (1989).

Harker, J. "The Whole Truth about Whole Language Instruction." In *Canadian Journal of English Language Arts*. Vol. 12, no. 1-2 (1989).

Mosenthal, P. "The Whole Language Approach: Teachers between a Rock and a Hard Place." In *The Reading Teacher*. Vol. 42, no. 8 (1989).

Ohanian, S. "Who's Afraid of Old Mother Hubbard?" In *New Advocate*. Vol. 3, no. 1 (1990).

Paulet, R. "The Whole Language Approach: Will It Be Used in Quebec and Manitoba?" In *English Quarterly*. Vol. 17, no. 4 (1984).
Reutzel, D.R. & Hollingsworth, P.M. "Whole Language and the Practitioner." In *Academic Therapy*. Vol. 23, no. 4 (1988).
Shannon, P. "The Struggle for Control of Literacy Lessons." In *Language Arts*. Vol. 66, no. 6 (1989).
Rich, S. "Restoring Power to Teachers: The Impact of Whole Language." In *Language Arts*. Vol. 62, no. 7 (1985).
Turnbull, C. "Three-Dimensional Teaching." In *Canadian Journal of English Language Arts*. Vol. 12, no. 1-2 (1989).
Yates, B. "Changing Attitudes." In *Canadian Journal of English Language Arts*. Vol. 12, no. 1-2 (1989).

WHOLE LANGUAGE JOURNEYS: PERSONAL ACCOUNTS

Edelsky, C. et. al. "Hookin' Em in the Start of School in a Whole Language Classroom." In *Anthropology and Education Quarterly*. Vol. 14, no. 4 (1983).
Griffith, P. & Klesius, J. "A Whole Language Flight Plan: An Interview with Three Teachers." In *Reading Horizons*. Vol. 30, no. 2 (1990).
Kamler, B. "Research Update: One Child, One Teacher, One Classroom: The Story of One Piece of Writing." In *Language Arts*. Vol. 57, no. 6 (1980).
Laurin, M.A. "Reading Reversal." In *Momentum*. Vol. 19, no. 2 (1988).
Newman, J. "Learning to Teach by Uncovering Our Assumptions." In *Language Arts*. Vol. 64, no. 7 (1987).
Newman, J. "Sharing Journals: Conversational Mirrors for Seeing Ourselves as Learners, Writers, and Teachers." In *English Education*. Vol. 20, no. 3 (1988).

THE READING-WRITING CONNECTION

Anderson-Inman, L. "Enhancing the Reading-Writing Connection: Classroom Application." In *The Writing Notebook*. Vol. 7, no. 3 (1990).
Collins, C. "The Power of Expressive Writing in Reading Comprehension." In *Language Arts*. Vol. 62, no. 1 (1985).
Crowell, D.C. et. al. "Emerging Literacy: Reading-Writing Experiences in a Kindergarten Classroom." In *The Reading Teacher*. Vol. 40, no. 2 (1986).

DeGroff, L. "Developing Writing Processes with Children's Literature." In *New Advocate*. Vol. 2, no. 2 (1989).
Graves, D.H. & Hansen, J. "The Author's Chair." In *Language Arts*. Vol. 60, no. 2 (1983).
Rhodes, L.K. "I Can Read! Predictable Books as Resources for Reading and Writing Instruction." In *The Reading Teacher*. Vol. 34, no. 5 (1981).
Smith, F. "Reading like a Writer." In *Language Arts*. Vol. 60, no. 5 (1983).

TEACHING WRITING

Bode, B. "Dialogue Journal Writing." In *The Reading Teacher*. Vol. 42, no. 8 (1989).
Calkins, L.M. "When Children Want to Punctuate: Basic Skills Belong in Context." In *Language Arts*. Vol. 57, no. 5 (1980).
Edelsky, C. & Smith, K. "Is That Writing — or Are Those Marks Just a Figment of Your Curriculum?" In *Language Arts*. Vol. 61, no. 1 (1984).
Gunderson, L. & Shapiro, J. "Whole Language Instruction: Writing in First Grade." In *The Reading Teacher*. Vol. 41, no. 4 (1988).
Hajek, E. "Whole Language: Sensible Answers to the Old Problems." In *Momentum*. Vol. 15, no. 2 (1984).
Parini, J. "The More They Write, the More They Write." In *The New York Times*. (July 30, 1989).

EMERGENT LITERACY

Cohn, M. "Observations of Learning to Read and Write Naturally." In *Language Arts*.Vol. 58, no. 5 (1981).
Heald-Taylor, B.G. "How to Use Predictable Books for K-2 Language Arts Instruction." In *The Reading Teacher*. Vol. 40, no. 7 (1987).
Heald-Taylor, B.G."Scribble in First Grade Writing." In *The Reading Teacher*. Vol. 38, no. 1 (1984).
Klein A. and Schickedanz, J. "Preschoolers Write Messages and Receive Their Favorite Books." In *Language Arts*. Vol. 57, no. 7 (1980).
Mavrogenes, N.A. "What Every Reading Teacher Should Know about Emergent Literacy." In *The Reading Teacher*. Vol. 40, no. 2 (1986).

Morrow, L.M. "Retelling Stories: A Strategy for Improving Young Children's Comprehension, Concept of Story Structure, and Oral Language Complexity." In *Elementary School Journal*. Vol. 85, no. 5 (1985).
Smardo, F.A. "Using children's Literature to Clarify Science Concepts in Early Childhood Programs." In *The Reading Teacher*. Vol. 36, no. 3 (1982).
Weir, B. "A Research Base for Prekindergarten Literacy Programs." In *The Reading Teacher*. Vol. 42, no. 7 (1989).

LEARNING TO USE LITERATURE IN THE CLASSROOM

Burchby, M. "Literature and Whole Language." In *New Advocate*. Vol. 1, no. 2 (1988).
Cole, A. "What Do You Notice?" In *The Reading Teacher*. Vol. 42, no. 4 (1989).
Cooter, R. "Blending Whole Language and Basal Reader." In *Reading Horizons*. Vol. 29, no. 4 (1989).
Corman, C. "Bibliotherapy — Insight for the Learning Handicapped." In *Language Arts*. Vol. 52, no. 7 (1975).
Craddock, S. & Halpern, H. "Developmental Listening in a Whole Language Classroom." In *Canadian Journal of English Language Arts*. Vol. 11, no. 1 (1988).
Cullinan, B. "Books in the Classroom." *Horn Book Magazine*. Vol. 62, no. 6 (1986).
Farris, P. "From Basal Reader to Whole Language: Transition Tactics." In *Reading Horizons*. Vol. 30, no. 1 (1989).
Ferguson, P. "Whole Language: A Global Approach to Learning." In *Instructor*. Vol. 97, no. 9 (1988).
Goodman, K. "Beyond Basal Readers: Taking Charge of Your Own Teaching." In *Learning*. Vol. 16, no. 2 (1987).
Harp, B. "When the Principal Asks: Why Don't You Ask Comprehension Questions?" In *The Reading Teacher*. Vol. 42, no. 8 (1989).
Harper, J. "The Teacher-Librarian's Role in Literature-Based Reading and Whole Language Programs." In *Emergency Librarian*. Vol. 17, no. 2 (1989).
Halpern, H. "Contemporary Canadian Children's Literature for the Intermediate Grades: A Whole Language Approach." In *Reading /Canada Lecture*. Vol. 5, no. 4 (1987).
Lamme, L. "Illustratorship: A Key Facet of Whole Language Instruction. In *Childhood Education*. Vol. 66, no. 2 (1989).

Lindberg, B. "Teaching Literature: The Process Approach." In *Journal of Reading*. Vol. 31, no. 8 (1988).
Mason, J. & Au, K. *Reading Instruction for Today*. 2nd Edition. Glenview, Illinois: Scott Foresman, 1990.
Morrow, L. "Inner-City Children's Recreational Reading." In *The Reading Teacher*. Vol. 41, no. 3 (1987).
Slaughter, H. "Indirect and Direct Teaching in a Whole Language Program." In *The Reading Teacher*. Vol. 42, no. 1 (1988).
Spiegel, D. "Content Validity of Whole Language Teachers." In *The Reading Teacher*. Vol. 43, no. 2 (1989).
Tunnell, M. & Jacobs, J. "Using 'Real' Books: Research Findings on Literature Based Reading Instruction." In *The Reading Teacher*. Vol. 42, no. 7 (1989).

SPELLING INSTRUCTION

Gentry, R. "An Analysis of Developmental Spelling in GNYS AT WRK." In *The Reading Teacher*. Vol. 36, no. 2 (1982).
Green, M. "Spelling within One School's Whole Language Framework." In *Australian Journal of Reading*. Vol. 11, no. 1 (1988).
James, M. "Self-Selected Spelling." In *Academic Therapy*. Vol. 21, no. 5 (1986).
Marsh, G. et. al. "The Development of Strategies in Spelling." *Cognitive Processes in Spelling*. Edited by Uta Frith. New York: Academic Press, 1980.
Norris, J. "Facilitating Developmental Changes in Spelling." In *Academic Therapy*. Vol. 25, no. 1 (1989).

WHOLE LANGUAGE AND SPECIAL POPULATIONS

Bolte, A. "Our Language Routine: Reading Together and Loving It." In *Perspectives for Teachers of the Hearing Impaired*. Vol. 5, no. 5 (1987).
Bolte, A. "Using Themes as the Building Blocks for Learning." In *Perspectives for Teachers of the Hearing Impaired*. Vol. 8, no. 1 (1989).
Brand, S. "Learning through Meaning." In *Academic Therapy*. Vol. 24, no. 3 (1989).
Corman, C. "Bibliotherapy — Insight for the Learning Handicapped." In *Language Arts*. Vol. 52, no. 7 (1975).

Ford, M. & Ohlhausen, M. "Tips from Reading Clinicians for Coping with Disabled Readers in Regular Classrooms." In *The Reading Teacher*. Vol. 42, no. 1 (1988).
Ganapole, S. "Reading and Writing for the Gifted: A Whole Language Perspective." In *Roeper Review*. Vol. 11, no. 2 (1988).
Hollingsworth, P. & Reutzel, R. "Whole Language with L.D. Children. In *Academic Therapy*. Vol. 23, no. 5 (1988).
Malicky, G. & Norman, C. "Whole Language: Applications to Special Education." In *Canadian Journal of English Language Arts*. Vol. 11, no. 3 (1988).
Oberlin, K. & Shugarman, S. "Implementing the Reading Work-Shop with Middle School L.D. Readers." In *Journal of Reading*. Vol. 32, no. 8 (1989).
Wicklund, L. "Shared Poetry. A Whole Language Experience Adapted for Remedial Readers." In *The Reading Teacher*. Vol. 42, no. 7 (1989).

EVALUATION

Bailey, J. et. al. "Problem-Solving Our Way to Alternative Evaluation Procedures." In *Language Arts*. Vol. 65, no. 4 (1988).
Black, J.K. "Those 'Mistakes' Tell Us a Lot." In *Language Arts*. Vol. 57, no. 5 (1980).
D'Angelo, K. "Correction Behavior: Implications for Reading Instruction." In *The Reading Teacher*. Vol. 35, no. 4 (1982).
Froese, V. "Language Assessment: What We Do and What We Should Do!" In *Canadian Journal of English Language Arts*. Vol. 11, no. 1 (1988).
Goodman, K.S. "Kid Watching: An Alternative to Testing." In *National Elementary Principals Journal*. 1988, Vol. 7, no. 4 (1988).
Harp, B. "When You Do Whole Language Instruction, How Will You Keep Track of Reading and Writing Skills?" In *The Reading Teacher*. Vol. 42, no. 2 (1988).

WHOLE LANGUAGE AND THE ARTS

Harp, B. "When the Principal Asks: Why Are Your Kids Singing during Reading Time?" In *The Reading Teacher*. Vol. 41, no. 4 (1988).
Mersereau, Y. et.al. "Dancing on the Edge." In *Language Arts*. Vol. 66, no. 2 (1989).

Children's Book Council Staff. Children's Books: Awards and Prizes. New York: Children's Book Council, 1985.
Children's Books in Print. New York: R.R. Bowker (Published annually).
Commire, A. *Something about the Author: Facts and Pictures about Contemporary Authors and Illustrators of Books for Young People.* Vol. 57. Detroit: Gale Research, 1989.
Cuddigan M. & Hanson, M.B. *Growing Pains: Helping Children Deal with Everyday Problems through Reading.* Chicago: American Library Association, 1988.
Dreyer, S. *The Bookfinder: A Guide to Children's Literature about the Needs and Problems of Youth Aged 2-15.* Circle Pines, Minnesota: American Guidance Service, 1989.
Gillespie J.T. & Gilbert, C.B. *Best Books for Children: Preschool through the Middle Grades.* 3rd Edition. New York: R.R. Bowker, 1985.
Holtze, S. (Ed.) *The Sixth Book of Junior Authors and Illustrators.* New York: N.W.Wilson, 1989.
Huck, C., Helpler S. & Hickman, J. *Children's Literature in the Elementary School.* 4th Edition. New York: Holt, Rinehart & Winston, 1987.
Kimmel, M. & Segal, E. *For Reading Out Loud: A Guide to Sharing Books with Children.* New York: Delacorte, 1988.
Landsberg, M. *Reading for the Love of It: Best Books for Young Readers.* New York: Prentice-Hall, 1987.
Lima C. & Lima, J. *A to Zoo: Subject Access to Children's Picture Books.* 3rd Edition. New York: R.R. Bowker, 1989.
Rudman, M. *Children's Literature: An Issues Approach.* 2nd Edition. Columbus, Ohio: Merrill, 1987.
Sutherland, Z., Monson, D. & Arbuthnot, M.H. *Children and Books.* 8th Edition. Glenview, Illinois: Scott, Foresman, 1991.
Trelease, J. *The New Read-Aloud Handbook.* 2nd Edition. New York: Penguin, 1989.
VanMeter, V. *American History for Children and Young Adults: An Annotated Bibliographic Index.* Englewood, Colorado. Libraries Unlimited, 1990.
Wilson, G. & Moss, J. *Books for Children: A Guide for Parents and Librarians.* New York: R.R. Bowker, 1988.

VIDEOTAPES

Theory and Practice in Two Meaning-Centered Classrooms. Carole Edelsky, 1984 (Available from Richard C. Owen).
The Writing Workshop: A World of Difference. Lucy Calkins and Shelly Harwayne, 1988 (Available from Heinemann).
The Authoring Cycle: Read Better, Write Better, Reason Better. Jerome Harste, 1987 (Available from Heinemann).
A Day in the Life of Mrs. Wishy Washy. San Diego, California: The Wright Group, 1990.
Learning through Literature: Grades K-3. New York: Scholastic.
Learning through Literature: Grades 4-6. New York: Scholastic
Big Books: Practical Strategies. New York: Scholastic.
Natural Language Learning. New York: Scholastic.

Early Childhood Organizations

Association for Childhood Educational International
11141 Georgia Avenue, Suite 200
Wheaton, MD 20902
Publishes: *Child Development*

National Association for the Education of Young Children
1834 Connecticut Avenue, N.W.
Washington, DC 20009
Publishes: *Young Children*

Professional Organizations

International Reading Association
800 Barksdale Road
P.O. Box 8139
Newark, DE 19714-8139
Publishes: *The Reading Teacher* and *Reading Research Quarterly*

National Council of Teachers of English
1111 Kenyon Road
Urbana, IL 61801
Publishes: *Language Arts*

Whole Language Umbrella — United States
Debbie Manning
4848 N. Fruit
Fresno, CA 93705

Whole Language Umbrella — Canada
Lorraine Krause
257 Beaconsfield Blvd.
Beaconsfield, Quebec H9W 4A5

TAWL (Teachers Applying Whole Language)
For information about the group nearest you, contact the Whole Language Umbrella.

CAWL (Children and Whole Language)
Carol Anne Ingle
Edmonton Public Schools Centre for Education
One Kingsway
Edmonton, Alberta T5H 4G9

Whole Language Newsletters

Dialogue
Center for Applied Linguistics
1118 22 Street NW
Washington, DC 10037

Teacher's Networking: The Whole Language Newsletter
Richard C. Owen Publishers
135 Katonah Ave.
Katonah, NY 10536

The Web
Ohio State University
Room 20, Ramseyer Hall
29 W Woodruff
Columbus, OH 43210

Whole Language Newsletter
Scholastic Canada
123 Newkirk Road
Richmond Hill, Ontario L4C 3G5

Whole Language Special Interest Group of IRA Newsletter
WLSIG
2801 West Broadway #F6
Columbus, MO 65203

Whole Language Teacher Support Groups

Whole Language Umbrella Information Clearinghouse
Charla Lau
P.O. Box 721326
Berkley, MI 48072

International Reading Association Whole Language Special Interest Group (WLSIG)
Paulette Whitman
R.R.#1
Lawrencetown
Annapolis County, Nova Scotia B0S 1M0

THE PIPPIN TEACHER'S LIBRARY

The titles in this series are designed to provide a forum for interpreting, in clear, straightforward language, current issues and trends affecting education. Teachers are invited to share — in their own voice — the insights, wisdom and knowledge they have developed out of their professional experiences.

Submissions for publication are welcomed. Manuscripts and proposals will be reviewed by members of the Pippin Teacher's Library Editorial Advisory Board, chaired by Lee Gunderson, PhD, of the University of British Columbia.

Written submissions should be directed to:
Editorial Director
Pippin Publishing Limited
150 Telson Road
Markham, Ontario
Canada
L3R 1E5